WOMEN IN MODERN INDIAN HISTORY

WOMEN IN MODERN INDIAN HISTORY

SUGAM ANAND

ANAMIKA PUBLISHERS & DISTRIBUTORS (P) LTD.
4697/3, 21A, Ansari Road, Daryaganj, New Delhi-110 002
Phones: 23281655, 23270239; Fax: 011-27868035
e-mail: anamikapublishers@yahoo.co.in

First Published, 2010

ISBN 978-81-7975-324-8

PRINTED IN INDIA

Published by Anamika Publishers & Distributors (P) Ltd., 4697/3, 21A, Ansari Road, Daryaganj, New Delhi - 110 002, Typeset and printed by Shivani Computers, Shahdara, Delhi - 110 093.

Contents

Preface

The present work entitled, 'Women in Modern Indian History' is the outcome of my curiosity and sincere efforts to study and understand the aspirations and determinations of the modern Indian women. They made efforts to change their socio-economic status and position in the light of the new liberal currents of the 19th century renaissance. Their gradual development began with the logical thoughts of the reformers and social thinkers who felt that for the attainment of freedom and self-government in the country, the women must be liberated enough to shoulder the new responsibilities in free India. Women welcomed the fresh fragrance of the new education and readily absorbed it in their lifestyle and other social ends. The outworn traditions were willingly discarded by them, especially in the urban regions. They emerged as individuals "nationally important and socially useful." They daringly crossed every hurdle on their way to their emancipation. They swiftly marched ahead on the road to plenty, progress, and prosperity for themselves as well as for their nation.

My intense study of women's history began a few years back. My recent book *Bhartiya Itihas Mein Nari* won a prestigious award from Uttar Pradesh Hindi Sansthan, Lucknow. It certainly gave to me enough incentive to explore further the Gender history of India. My Ph.D. thesis entitled History of Empress Nurjahan Begum had been related to this field. It was published in 2001. I have translated my mother's book 'Social Transformation of U.P. Women', which she completed as an S.R.F. Project of I.C.H.R., New Delhi. All this provided me with lot of opportunities to enlarge the panorama of my study of Indian feminism and socio-economic status of women in modern India. I found that Indian feminism was quite different from the feminist movements of other countries.

Modern Indian women are educated, cultured and self-reliant, yet they stick to the age-old ideals and values of life. The western concepts of feminism did not appeal to them. The Indian government attempted not only to enact legal reforms for their upliftment but also made it a practical reality. The women of rural India have sincerely worked in different fields of life. They work in the agricultural sectors and cottage industries. Modern Indian women are working in large numbers in different respectable professions. Women's role in the national struggle as well as their participation in the reconstruction of the country has really been amazing. They have distinguished themselves in all walks of life. The story of their regeneration and their participation in the task of nation building has been specially taken up in the present work.

I am obliged to my mother Prof. Pratima Asthana, who has been a pioneer in research and writing, in the field of gender history. Besides research and writing, she has also worked through many organizations for the cause of womens' upliftment. I am also grateful to all those who have contributed to women's history and brought to light the contribution of modern Indian women in a new setting and background. I am obliged to Prof. Jafri, HOD, Delhi University for his ready help and advice.

I humbly dedicate this book to the Holy Feet of the Almighty who showered His special grace on me to complete this project, despite all my pre-occupations in the University programmes and academic projects.

1st January 2010 SUGAM ANAND

1. Looking Back

Indian women displayed a bright and brilliant record of achievements during the Vedic age of Indian history. They were known not only for their accomplishments but also for their creative and noble contribution to the society. They represented the highest aspirations of the race. The Vedic period represents the golden age especially with reference to women's elevated status in society. It has rightly been asserted that the position of women in any society or country provides the real indication of its socio-cultural and spiritual standards. In the Vedic period, they fully imbibed the cultural values of this ancient land.

The Vedic women enjoyed an equal status with men by dint of their merit and intellectual maturity, they could earn a rare veneration in society. They enjoyed full freedom for spiritual progress and intellectual development. The Aryans, who were engaged in the arduous task of political expansion in India, desired the co-operation of their women in every walk of life. The women performed their duties at home and outside perfectly well. They worked in the political institutions of the period and successfully acted as members of the political institutions like 'Sabha' and 'Samiti'.

The Atharva Veda recommends a ritual for ensuring the birth of a scholarly daughter. The girl child was not unwelcome in the Vedic houses. Daughters were also initiated in the Vedic studies and were allowed to lead a life devoted to learning, self-control and discipline. Women gained eminence in composing sacred Vedic 'richas'. They served as teachers, debaters, poets and spiritualists and excelled in education and learning. The pursuit of spiritualism made them Brahma-Vadinis. The daughters were married at a mature age and they had full freedom in the choice of their husbands. From the solemn affirmations and promises mutually made by the bride and the bridegroom, it appears that monogamy largely prevailed in Vedic society except among the rich and royal classes. The wife was the husband's companion in weal and woe, the manager and mistress of the household and the real partner in all his activities—temporal and spiritual. With a high sense of responsibility and education, the women were regarded as the joint owners of the household, and they efficiently managed the family. They were free to attend and visit public assemblies and social entertainments. They participated in the programmes of discussion organized in mixed gatherings. They were active participants in the work of agriculture and they co-operated with men in the manufacture of bows, arrows, and other tool and instruments. The quick development of cottage industries could be possible only through active cooperation interest of the women folk.

They worked mainly in agriculture and textile industry. They also contributed to the work of pubic utility. They worked hard and displayed their merit in the intellectual fields. They were the singers of the dawn and composers of Vedic hymns. After the Vedic age, a gradual deterioration set in their status and position in the society. The injunctions of Manu, on which rested the fabric of Hindu society deprived them of the right to education. The practice of Upanayana for the daughters was stopped. They were married early and their husbands were authorized to be their 'gurus'. They were not allowed to touch the religious texts and join the higher studies. They were reduced almost to the status of

Shudras. They were gradually forced to be inferior to men in education and culture. Alleging their temperament to be fickle and emotional, Manu propounded the theory of the perpetual tutelage for women in the family and society.

The social norms and traditions merged the individuality of the wife into that of her husband and the male members of the family who were considered superior to her. A rigorous discipline was prescribed for the widows. Child marriages, polygamy and suppression were allowed by the law-givers. Chastity and motherhood were adored in the family. It was believed that the women were not able to take independent decisions themselves so they must always remain dependent on the male members of the family.

With the coming of the two reform-religions, Buddhism and Jainism, women felt some relief. They were allowed to be 'nuns' and join the separate monasteries for spiritual pursuits. They wrote the 'Therigathas' and expressed their pain and sorrow in poetry. However, even as members of the ascetic order, they were not considered to be equal to the Bhikshus, but rather subordinates.

Women led a happy but deprived life in the family. They were held in high veneration as mothers. Their right over Stri-dhana remained secure through out the period. Some valiant queens were known in the Rajput period for their valour and merit. They continued their intellectual and spiritual pursuits. Some of them had the command over swords, and many of them were daring enough to perform 'Jauhar' when their husbands were defeated in the decisive wars. After the advent of Islam, the Hindu society became more rigid in its attitude towards women. The influx of the warrior Turks and the terror they struck, led the Hindus to be more strict in social norms, as the women were forcibly seized by the invaders.

Under the circumstances, the Hindus forsook their relationship with their daughters or sisters who were looted away by the aliens. Many heroic women specially the Rajput women preferred to jump into the fire than to fall into the grip of the impious hands. The Hindus, as an expediency measure, curtailed all freedom of their women folk. Sanctions were imposed on them that became a social evil in the long run.

Women were kept under strict control and seclusion. For their safety, the Hindu law givers adopted the practice of child marriages. The customs of polygamy and unequal marriages began to prevail at large. The new custom of infanticide was invented and the girl child was killed as soon as she was born. The fate of a Hindu widow became miserable under the custom of tonsure and strict moral sanctions. The practice of Sati found favour with the ruling classes and the people of upper castes and classes.

The Bhakti movement in medieval India had brought some relief to women. The Saints and Sufis delivered a message of love and equity in society. Women joined the cult of Bhakti. Some of them discarded purdah, shunned the traditional rigidities and distinguished themselves as symbols of piety, truth and devotion. The impact of Bhakti movement, however, was not lasting.

The devotional cults stood for the right of women to religious worship. One, however, feels that even their efforts proved in vain. During the Mughal period, seclusion of women was taken to be a symbol of social honour and etiquette. However, women who belonged to the cultivating and labouring classes did not observe purdah and worked freely in the rural fields and different cottage industries.

Despite the instructions of the prophet to treat the women with love and honour, they came to be considered as a burden in Islam. The customs of early marriage and dowry were adopted by them, perhaps, on account of their ultimate Indianization and their intermingling with the Hindus. The rich men practised polygamy. Akbar had ordered that the man of ordinary means must not have more than one wife. The miserable women who were divorced, were forced to practise prostitution. They adopted the practice of singing and dancing in the urban regions to earn their livelihood.

The practice of remarriage and divorce among the Muslims created complications in a family where widows came with children from their first marriage. Hindus with the exception of the ruling and the wealthy classes, were by and large monogamous. Hindu women did not believe in re-marriage after widowhood and this caused the popularity of 'Sati' which was then regarded as the object of highest veneration. The 'Sati Chauras', found all around in the country testify to this fact.

Female education, gradually, became extinct in society, except in the ruling classes who provided their daughters the opportunities for the cultivation of their mental discipline. Still, many social taboos and constraints were imposed upon them. Women tried to be happy and contented. Akbar held the Hindu women in great admiration and he often said in public that they were sometimes neglected even though they had proved to be "flaming torches of love and fellowship" Jahangir also admired Hindu women for their single-minded devotion and fidelity. Meera Bai, a great devotee of Lord Krishna, revolted against the unjust social traditions. She exemplified the ideals of truth and devotion. Nurjahan outlined a new work culture among the women of the royal harem and taught them to be self reliant. Many women worked under her inspiration in the royal *'Karkhanas'* of dress-designing and manufacturing rose scents which her mother Asmat Begum invented.

Yet, the fact remains that the majority of women presented the sight of "dumb driven cattle." Under the stress of new-fangled *Shastrik* injunctions, they fell prey to many an abhorrent customs and dead usages. Majority of them were uneducated and ignorant. One sided morality was encouraged in society where a man was free to torture the weak women and discard her.

At the advent of British rule in India, the evil of infanticide prevailed mainly in Rajasthan and Punjab. The Jats of western U.P. and the Muslim Saiyyads also practised this crime.

With the exception of some Rajputs and Zamindar families, society in general had strange notions about female education. They believed that if a girl was taught to read and write, she was sure to become a widow. Such prejudices perpetuated illiteracy and ignorance among the women. Lack of education led to their indifference and dislike towards the cultivation of fine arts. Music and dance were regarded as the pursuit of "dancing-girls." The folk songs sung on ceremonial occasions were of a low order. The *'kothas'* in various cities became the centre of evening entertainment for the rich men. The female exploitation thus increased day by day. The custom of early marriages gave a rude shock to the physical, intellectual and spiritual development of the fair sex. The girl-child from the moment of her birth to death underwent tortures and life-long suffering as child-wife and as child-mother. Many superstitious feelings were perpetuated by the ignorant women themselves. The premature marriage and maternity resulted in increase in the death-rate of the mothers and the infants both. Having no concept of health or hygiene, the women suffered from many deadly diseases. No proper medical facility was made available to them except in some rich households. The poor women suffered constantly without any remedy or relief.

Strict seclusion was observed by the upper class women of both the communities. Women were segregated in the back or the *zanana* apartments. Houses of the poor people had dark and dingy rooms where women passed their time in cooking, cleaning and child-bearing under very unhealthy conditions. The wealthy people had separate *Zanana* apartments where "the women lay condemned to a life-long prison, a pathetic figure with feeble health; her naturally keen senses being dulled through inaction without the light of self-knowledge." There was nothing to illuminate their vision and they were steeped in deep ignorance and prejudices. The curse of polygamy aggravated their agony all the more. Though legally permitted only in the case of first wife's barrenness, men practised polygamy without any restraint. Among the middle class Hindus, polygamy did not exist as a rule. However, the *Kuleen* Brahmins of Bengal observed this practice so freely that sometimes they married more than a hundred girls. Muslims were polygamous, and their women had to undergo severe tortures on this account. They could be very easily divorced by their husbands.

The Sati-stones belonging to the 17th and 18th centuries found in almost all regions of the country, show that "the Sati custom was frequently followed by the commoners as well." During this period, the practice of Sati had become very popular in Bengal, especially among the Brahmins.

The ban on remarriage of widows, the rigorous discipline and strict austerity enforced upon them, made the women's life a den of miseries. The presence of widows was regarded inauspicious on festive occasions. The priests had prescribed for them the custom of tonsure and practice of extreme simplicity in food and dress. Some, however, found the ideals too difficult to follow. The path of righteousness was imperative for them. Falling prey to odd circumstances, they had no other option than to join the *'Kothas'*, when they were accepted by none. The social rigidity, child-marriages with its evil consequences, child-widows, the social taboos involved in widow re-marriages created a new class of women, whom they designated as 'fallen'. About the Hindu widows, it was written in the proceedings of Legislative Council, "Not only must she see no man; she must also avoid every approach to ease, and pleasure. She must neglect the care of her person, must wear no ornaments; her hair must be shaven. She must not anoint her body; and her dress must be coarse and dirty. The use of any kind of conveyance was prohibited for them. She must not eat in bed. Her food was coarse and ordinary both in quantity and quality and she must not take more than a single coarse meal a day." However, widows from the lower castes could remarry and avoid all censures.

The Stri-dhana was legally interpreted in liberal terms but women were generally excluded from succession to property. Ultimately it made them fully dependent. Restrained by customs they could not play any constructive role in society. The only option left open to them was that of marriage. In the lower sections of society, women worked in fields and were engaged in other manual labour. They were however kept under watch. The association of dancing girls and professional singers with temples, meant a silent approval of their physical exploitation by priests. They were invited to entertain the gathering on ceremonial occasions. The use of liquors and intoxicants were often a common feature of these celebrations. In many parts of the country, especially in Punjab, U.P. and Bengal, the dancing girls enjoyed public favour. "They moved far more freely in society than the respectable women of any civilized people." The dancing girls had a very detrimental effect on people. Many a family's happiness was ruined and complete estrangement between the husband and wife occurred when the husband went under the influence of "dancing-girls."

At the advent of the British rule, the moral standard of temple-dancing had shamefully declined. In Madras, the '*devdasis*' often led an immoral life in the name of forged religion. They were forced to satiate the lust of temple priests in a degrading manner. In Maharashtra, many unfortunate girls were dedicated to the temples to dance before the idols. They had to remain unmarried and were called *Muralis*. The young *Muralis* became professional dancers for the rich aristocracy. In their old age, they grew weak and passed their life with great difficulty. The Vaishnavite sects in Bengal, and western parts of U.P. had dancing girls in temples and the poor women were forced to satiate the lust of the temple priests, when they moved in groups from one holy pace to another. In western and central India, the professional singers and dancers were called *Bairagis* and *Kalawantins.* They were invited by the temple priests and the wealthy nobles to present their programme of music and dance. The low taste of the people became responsible for the cultural stagnation and moral bankruptcy of the then society. In the 18th century, dead customs, blind faith, ritualism and traditionalism governed the socio-religious life of the women. Identifying superstition with the very style of living, the priests sublimated the lowest activities into sacraments. They fearlessly visited distant places of pilgrimages and the unescorted females were exploited by them on the way.

In the Tirths, the women bathed in the rivers publicly. They hankered after 'Siddhi' and 'Shakti' and believed in witchcraft, Tantrik *kriya* and the magic of evil spirits. They wandered often in graveyards and *Shamshans.* They strictly adhered to the extremities of religion and felt no reluctance even in throwing their own illegitimate children into the rivers. Under the evil influence of the so-called Brahmin priests, they cruelly sacrificed animals and children at the alter of tantrik gods.

It is quite strange that the common Indian women nourished the ideals of *Sita* and *Savitri.* They did not lack in the spirit of self-sacrifice and submission, tolerance and nobility, purity and piety. They were devoted to their families and children and lived under the shelter of elders. The shining image of Vedic womanhood, well rooted in ancient Indian religious texts gradually changed, and a general degradation set in.

In short, in the early dawn of civilization, Indians had

evolved a balanced philosophy of life and assigned the women an honoured status in society. Presenting a synthesis between the material and the spiritual aspects of life, they provided the women with the key to unlock their finest capabilities and genius. Gradually, this unique balance disappeared under the instructions of male law-givers and the increasing complexities of the social life underwent a radical change. Instead of honour, the women became the object of pleasure. Even the saints condemned them as impediments in the path of religious progress and they closed their eyes towards their degrading status.

When the system of slavery was introduced in India, the defeated race had to perform all essential services and the women who were once honoured for their useful work stopped to be productive members of society. Their position was, therefore, reduced to a secondary and subordinate level. The inclusion of the non-Aryan wife in the family, who did not possess the knowledge of Vedic rituals, became an important cause, responsible for the general degradation of women. In order to assign equal status to every wife and maintain domestic peace, all the women were declared ineligible for religious studies and Yajnas. The women's role in Vedic rites and mantras became formal. When the socio-religious laws and customs grew complex, many false notions of touch and smell sprang up in society. Women naturally could not escape the burden of religious taboos. During menstruation and in the period of child bearing, women were regarded as impious and untouchables. They were not allowed to participate in religious worship. As time rolled on, the very idea of their active participation in religious rites was altogether forgotten.

The Indian society determined the status of women by the verdicts of the seers and sages who codified the prevalent rules. It was very unfortunate that after the Vedic period, rationalism and the spirit of enquiry ceased to inspire the social thinkers and religious preachers. The Smriti writers like Manu, Yajnavalkya, Parashar and many others issued mandates to discontinue the practice of Upanayana for the daughters. The system of female education in the country received a rude shock due to such innovations. Women were forced to remain illiterate and ignorant. The jurists also burdened women's life with many social taboos culminating in evil customs. Under the circumstances, women had no other option than to succumb to the theory of their perpetual obedience and subjugation.

The invasion of Turks and the policy of loot and plunder which they adopted, the question before Rajputs in particular and other Hindus in general was that of saving the honour of their young females and to protect them. The family honour was identified with the chastity of women. As a result the social rules and norms towards women became more rigid than ever before. The devices which were adopted to protect them later became the reason of their degradation. No one ever questioned the blind laws depriving them of equality of status in society. As a result, they lost their self-consciousness and the urge for freedom and equality. They readily adopted the dangerous 'culture of silence'.

Rabindranath Tagore once wrote, "Our country lost its link with the innermost Truths of Truths in struggling against a crushing load of unreason, in abject slavery to circumstances. In social usage, in politics, in the realm of religion and art, we entered the zone of uncreative habit, of decadent tradition and we did not exercise our humanity."

With a general decay and degeneration, there ensued the stagnation of the social customs. In fact, the dark and dismal years of the 18th century, left their deepest mark on the degeneration of the status and position of women in India. The caste structure became rigid. The Brahmins, who professionally were hereditary priests, exercised considerable influence on society and became responsible for deepening the gloom that had already overcast the Indian women. With their traditional orthodox views and degenerated outlook, they made religion the handmaid of vice and folly. In the name of tradition they misguided the society to adopt a callous and inhuman attitude towards women. Women gradually lost their rightful place in society. A.S. Altekar concluded that, "Denied the benefits of education, brought up in the authoritarian atmosphere, having no awareness and self dependence, the status of women underwent a shocking change in India when the Britishers made this great land as their colony and crushed it under their imperialistic feet."

As every dark cloud has a silver lining, so there was the spark of new life for the women of India. Under the shadow of imperialism and colonialism in the 19th century, India suffered the economic exploitation of the British Raj and its discriminative machinery of centralized authoritarian rule. It was a much bigger and hazardous shock to the country. Yet, it was this corrupt and dishonest rule could open the flood gates of modern knowledge to the Indians at large.

The new education introduced by the British acquainted the Indians with western history, philosophy and science and technology. A country once renowned in history for the developed system of education at Nalanda, Taxila, Vikramsila and Vallabhi universities was granted a new environment by the western thinkers and philosophers. They were reminded of their own glorious past and decided to endeavour for the changes in their socio-political life. The Indian students felt an inner urge to pursue the gift of western education afresh. It is beyond doubt that the new education brought about a metamorphosis in the life of Indian women too. They could notice the changing hues and colours in their own life. The educated women decided to carve a better future for themselves as well as for their motherland.

2. The Dawn

From the gloom and darkness of the 18th century, there spontaneously emerged the bright golden rays of Indian Renaissance. The Indians felt the stir of the 19th century renaissance which promised them a socio-cultural transformation and a total change from 'old to new'. Under the British rule and its exploitative 'sceptre', the Indian outlook underwent a remarkable change due to the fruits of western scientific ideas and philosophy. A new educational set-up was opened up for them. English language and literature became the vehicle through which the new 'dawn' enlightened and inspired the urban Indians. The expectation of a new world order, based on liberalism, inspired them and they desired English education for their own regeneration. The Indians soon realised that for a country like India, the return to India's glorious past and the revival of their Vedic ideals were definitely required rather than mere aping of the western life-style. It was generally agreed that for a healthy social regeneration of the Indians, the best of the ancient values must be combined with the best elements of western scientific and logical thinking. Majority of the Indian thinkers supported this view and they became keen, not only for their own education but for the education of Indian women too. They stressed upon the British government through 'Press' to open girls' schools on an enormous scale and to extend all facilities to them for obtaining the 'new education'.

It was just a revolution that became discernible in all fields of socio-economic life of India. The Christian Missionaries were keen to spread their gospel in India. The imperialists allowed them to begin their religious propagation after 1813. The missionaries rapidly spread all over the country and started the mission of proselytization. Ignorant as the missionaries were in matters relating to Hindu religion, they vehemently attacked its socio-religious practices practised among the Hindus. The British had come as representatives of an alien civilization. They belonged to the governing class. They assumed an imaginary complex of being superior to the Indians and declared that it was with a 'civilizing zeal' that they came to work in this country.

In spite of many enthusiastic listeners, they could hardly find earnest seeker ready to embrace their faith. They had failed in convincing the higher classes and castes. They diverted their activities to the conversion of the untouchables and the deprived castes. With the object of the diffusion of the gospel, they started educational institutions in India. They opened orphanages, medical dispensaries and carried on an extensive propaganda of social reform and programme of famine relief. Assuring the converts of better prospects and position in society, they even offered them financial assistance and small jobs. Yet they failed to make any serious dent on Hinduism or Islam. Their work in the field of conversion, on the whole, did not prove encouraging enough. In the field of social service, they had a good record of achievements and their educational institutions introduced a new spirit of understanding and a better appreciation of life in the community. They gave an impetus to the emerging spirit of introspection and a search within among educated Indians. They carried on a rigorous reform propaganda especially about the low status of women in Hindu society. They openly criticized the evils of Sati, early marriage, polygamy, dowry, infanticide and temple-dancing etc. They condemned the seclusion of women and their colossal illiteracy. They exaggerated the defects in the Hindu Law of Inheritance. They mocked at the social inequity prevalent in India and published caricatures of women. They condemned Hindu gods in a highly objectionable style. They thought that Christianity could alone serve as the panacea to all ills and evils of the Indian society. The challenge was later taken up by the indigenous reformers who began to make a critical assessment of their own socio-religious customs and traditions. They launched a campaign against the social evils and infused the new rays of self criticism in the existing Hindu social structure. The outcome was a sincere statement of ethical values which recognized the need for basic reforms in the socio-economic life of India.

The missionaries sincerely tried to persuade the Government to abandon the indifferent policy towards the unjust customs prevalent in India. They collected information regarding particular cases of inhuman and barbarous customs. In the history of the country, for the first time, the Indians began to have an awareness about their own social backwardness and moral degeneration. They were determined to start socio-religious reform movements. N.S. Bose later pointed out that, "it required the challenge of Christian missionary activity to rouse Bengal from the deep slumber of ages."

The Serampore missionaries led by William Carey started a determined agitation against the custom of 'Sati'. A Memorandum was submitted to Lord Wellesley's government against the practice of Sati. They urged the government to take measures against this inhuman practice. They presented it to the British public, both at home and in India, in a forceful yet scholarly fashion, and thus prepared the setting in which government action became inevitable and the Sati abolition Act was passed in 1829.

They executed the work of imparting education to

Indians specially the women and established schools for them in 1819. They opened Girls' Day Schools, Orphan's Domestic Dwellings, and Domestic Teaching by the Governesses inside the houses of the upper class Indians. The Calcutta Juvenile Society and the Serampore Female Society made notable contribution in this field. The Ladies' Society for Native Female Education was formed in 1824 under the patronage of Lady Amherst which managed more than 30 girls' schools. The London Missionary Society and Church Missionary Society persuaded the people to shake off all prejudices against female education.

The Christian Missions opened a number of Girls' schools in Madras and Bombay Presidencies. Due to their denominational character, these schools could not attract females of the upper and middle strata of Indian society. The people of lower stratum who were a bit free of the social bondages, sent their daughters to the Missionary schools. They were awarded liberal prizes in cash and kind, yet the response in attendance remained poor. The activities of the Christian missionaries in the field of female education ultimately enlightened the Indian public opinion. The orthodox Hindus launched an opposition but the enlightened families realized the necessity and importance of female education. They began to take interest and offered their selfless services to open girls schools in various parts of the country.

It is a fact that the new ideas of renaissance enthused the educated Indians to realize the need of social reforms to be the foundation of new India. The government of the East India Company remained indifferent and did not think it proper to favour the activities of the missionaries to help the Indians. In 1800, David Hare, who settled at Calcutta, pursued the task of introducing western literature and science to the Indians. He made efforts to bring about a moral improvement among the natives of Bengal. The Charter of

1813 laid down that a sum of Rupees one lakh should be spent annually by the East India Company on education of Indians. Knowing about the welfare activities of the Missionaries, Lala Lajpat Rai once noted that, "there is now a network of social service agencies throughout India mainly due to the contact of the East with the West and on the pattern of Christian missionary's efforts." J.C. Marshaman opposed their activities on the ground, that these would interfere with the principles of Hindu religion which is known to have produced men of purest morality and strictest virtue.

For the betterment of education in India, a Committee of Public Instruction was set up to administer and to manage the provisional grants. The Company's officials did not think it proper to force the natives to study an alien language and literature. They decided to establish in 1823, the three colleges of Calcutta, Delhi and Agra with Sanskrit as the main subject of study.

Raja Rammohun Roy, the great reformer, protested against the establishment of the Sanskrit Colleges. He expressed the hope that the finances sanctioned in 1813 and 1823 should be better utilized in employing European teachers to instruct the natives of India in Mathematics, Natural Philosophy, Chemistry, Anatomy and other new sciences. The Committee of Public Instruction was sharply divided on the issue. Some of the members favoured that the natives should pursue their current course of instruction and endeavour to engraft European Sciences afterwards. The other group desired 'to devote all the available money to education through the medium of English in the hope and belief that the numbers affected through it, would consider the western culture as best in the world and might adopt it later. The knowledge would then gradually filter through the whole of society.' Many others like Elphinstone and Malcolm, non-members of the Committee, advocated to impart western knowledge in the Vernaculars, leaving English to be studied as a classical language by those who were disposed to pursue it.

Lord William Bentinck was greatly opposed to the idea of education through the Vernaculars. Macaulay's vehement rhetoric, was not based on any knowledge of Indian languages. He, however, carried the day against the Orientalists. In 1835, it was decided that "the great object of British Government ought to be the promotion of English literature and science among the natives of India and that all funds appropriated to education would best be employed in English education alone. Macaulay's objective was to create a class of persons who would be "Indian in blood and colour but English in tastes, in opinion, and in morals." It became clear that the discussion had weighed strongly in favour of English education." In fact, English education opened the floodgates of western ideas which almost overwhelmed the Indians in the beginning. On the immature young minds, who were drunk deep into the alien culture, the first reaction was of a deliberate revolt against the cherished Indian ideals.

The orthodox section of men were alarmed at the total wreck of Hindu society for which they held the English education solely responsible. The Wood's Despatch of 1854, co-ordinated the educational system on a national scale.

The system of higher education in English language provided India with a class of men imbued with social purposes and objectives. A new ideology suddenly burst forth upon the static life moulded for centuries by a fixed set of religious ideas and social conventions. While the British administration did little, if anything, to emancipate the Indian spirit or to extinguish the prejudices and to eradicate the ravages of ignorant customs and pernicious superstitions, it certainly provided the Indians with a critical attitude towards religion and a spirit of enquiry into the origin of state and society with a view to determining their proper progress. Very soon the educated Indians began the much awaited task of self introspection and improvement in their thought. The new education produced a feeling of like-mindedness among the people. It gave to India a common language for exchange of ideas and produced a sense of lingual unity in the country. It also enabled Indians to share the results of the great movements of other countries in the world. The spirit of scientific research and independent enquiry along with the importance of reason as the governing force in life, once again became the part and parcel of Indian attitude to life. Fresh elements of a new philosophy and the dynamics of a revolutionary thought became the spring source of India's transformation into a modern country. With a broad and rational outlook, the enlightened Indians proceeded to remove the social disabilities that existed for long. The ideas of liberalism, humanitarianism, progress and change, began to dominate the dim social scenario and the Indians who set forth to revive their indigenous cultural values, accepted useful social reforms in order to ameliorate, specially the women's lot. The women too were keen to be educated. After the English education armed them with a new knowledge and it broadened their outlook, they regained their long lost self-consciousness and attempted to change the socio-economic scenario. They began to compare their own restricted and overburdened life with the equal status and freedom enjoyed by the western women. They were determined to carve a new life for themselves.

Aware to their age-long sufferings at the hands of orthodox society, they desired to launch a crusade against the pernicious social evils, affecting them. They organized themselves into units to fight for their rights and to effectively play their distinctive role in shaping the country's destiny. They adopted the spirit of enquiry along with the importance of reason as the governing power in life. With fresh elements of a new and revolutionary thought, the new knowledge became the spring-source of India's transformation into a great land, equipped with healthy ideas of women's progress as individuals who were destined to play a significant role in the freedom struggle of India.

India's interaction with the 19th century renaissance resulted in the new awakening and the Indian women could not resist the temptation of being educated and enlightened. A new dawn awaited them and definitely what this awakening brought, was the natural outcome of the changing scenario. Renaissance in the Indian context stood for revival and restoration of ancient values and ideals. The women desired to adopt those very ideas and ideals which had once been the salient features of Indian culture specially the Vedic culture. They were inspired to regenerate themselves, sticking to their ancient values. They availed the opportunity of education and began to lead a better life. The new constructive urges made them worthy of respect and veneration of the then society. They gradually became self-reliant and some of them became able to take independent decisions for their family. Armed with modern education, they thought that they shall be able to cast off subjugation and misery. Though they silently suffered their inferior status, they gradually acquired the right to protest against the one-sided constraints and courageously laid the foundation of a mighty women's movement in a country like India. Many women's institutions sprang up with banners of protest and gradually women attained all that for which they had aspired once. They attained equal status in all fields of life. They attained the dignity and freedom which they had once enjoyed in the Vedic age of Indian history.

To sum up, the impact of West brought a new 'dawn' in India. The radiant rays of renaissance disturbed the dead equilibrium of the traditional life. Women were exposed to a totally new concept of themselves as transformed individuals, who in the long journey of life remained as 'socially useful and nationally needed'. The restlessness of women made them to derive benefits of western liberalism, utilitarianism and the new scientific inventions.

The women who were engaged in agriculture and small scale industries, could not avoid the wonderful impact of the new dawn. How queer it appears that before Lady Beilby left for England, she visited the *Zanana* of a few houses. The Indian women gave her a gold necklace to be presented to Her Excellency, Queen Victoria with a request that arrangements for female hospitals be made as early as possible to give relief to the females of India. The women working in factories and workshops, began to demand better service conditions and a cut in their hours of work.

An unending search began for the women of India to acquire their identity and worth. Their dreams started coming true, through their distinguished performance and wisdom. They displayed, in later years, a rare determination to serve the country with their 'will and might'.

3. Reformers' Zeal

From Rammohun Roy to Gandhi, almost all the reformers proved to be the change-makers and their insistence on reforms affected Indian women consistently with the changing time. They all wanted to give them their rightful place in society. With religious zeal and rational fervour, they advocated the necessity of social reforms in the country. They boldly dealt with the challenges thrown to them by the orthodox section of the Indian society. The reformers had a firm conviction that with the betterment of women's lot, the general progress and freedom of the entire country would follow. As such the women of India must be adorned with the rare virtues of Indian culture to play a positive role.

In fact, they aspired to revive the Vedic ideals of Indian womanhood. They inaugurated the most brilliant era of social reforms in India. Designated as the 'Father of Indian Renaissance', Raja Rammohun Roy was the first great champion of women's cause. He was born in 1774 and was brought up in a religious atmosphere. He was a scholar of Sanskrit, Arabic, Persian, Sanskrit and Bengali. He later studied English language and literature. He also learnt some Hebrew, Greek and Latin. He also studied the Upanishads and other Hindu scriptures. According to Rammohun, 'It was erroneous to consider women as weak in intellect and virtue and deficient in resolution, trust and self-control.' He led a successful campaign against the practice of 'Sati'. He petitioned to the Government and organized Vigilance committees to prevent 'Sati' rites when the widow was burnt alive on the pyre of the dead husband. He often used to personally visit the burning 'ghats' at Calcutta to dissuade the frenzied crowd and rescue the helpless victims. The conservatives opposed him tooth and nail. They formed an association known as 'Dharma Sabha' with the object of preventing the Government from legislating against Sati. Rammohun submitted another petition to the government in which he quoted from the holy scriptures and the injunctions of law-givers like Manu and Yajnavalkya in support of his views against Sati. He declared that 'to allow, to force, and to justify Sati amounted to the sin of female murder.' When Lord Bentinck enacted a legislation to abolish Sati in 1829, it was Rammohun's personal victory. He was also opposed to polygamy and considered it as a blot on the fair name of Hinduism. He had convinced the Governor General as well as the intellectuals of his logic against the crime of Sati. He wrote that, 'it was a crime to force a woman to commit Sati simply on the grounds of falsely attributed faults.... I am at a loss to conceive, how persons can reconcile themselves to the stigma of being accused of murdering the living widow. He extensively quoted from the ancient scriptures and stressed on the need of removing the property disabilities of women. In order to carry further the reform activities in an organized way, he founded the Brahmo Samaj in 1828. His utilitarian thought and liberal philosophy earned for him an enviable position, unparalleled in the annals of social reforms in India.

Another reformer was Debendra Nath Tagore who was born in 1817. He received his education in the Hindu College. He wanted to advance the cause of social, educational and cultural progress of the country. He supported the introduction of female education, re-marriage of Hindu widows and prevention of polygamy.

He established 'Samajonnati Bidhayini Suhrid Samiti'.

This organization attracted prominent public men who acquired its membership. He submitted a memorandum to the legislative Council for the removal of legal disabilities of remarried Hindu widows. He also appealed to the Council to open girls' schools in every quarter of the suburbs of Calcutta. He himself donated a large sum of money for the propagation of female education. Debendra Nath took up the unfinished task of Raja Rammohun Roy in the field of women's emancipation. Through Brahmo Samaj, he led a vigorous campaign for change through social reforms.

Born in 1820 in a Brahmin family, Ishwar Chandra Vidya Sagar was a brilliant scholar of Sanskrit. He inherited from his mother a broad and liberal outlook. He served the Fort William College as a lecturer in Sanskrit and then became the Principal of another College in Calcutta. He started a dynamic campaign in favour of widow remarriage in Bengal. He collected immense examples from Hindu holy scriptures to support his views and he wrote a book known as *Marriage of Hindu Widows*.

Ishwar Chandra declared that 'a total disregard of the Shastras and a careful observance of usages and practices were the sources of the irresistible stream of vices which had over-flown the country.' He exhorted upon his country-men to revive the practice of widow remarriage, as it was sanctioned in the Hindu scriptures.

He sent a petition to the Council signed by more than one thousand individuals in favour of property rights of the widows. His efforts came to fruition in 1856 when the Widow Re-marriage Act was passed by the Government even in the face of bitter opposition from the orthodox section led by Radhakant Deb.

Ishwar Chandra Vidya Sagar took an important part in the crusade against polygamy. He collected detailed information and data about the prevalence of this evil in Bengal. He also raised his voice against the practise of 'early marriage' and carried on an extensive propaganda to extend the age of consent to 'ten' years. Vidya Sagar was all out for the spread of female education in Bengal. He held an essay competition on "Utility of female Education." In the prize-distribution function, he invited Mr. Bethune who was a learned scholar and who spoke freely on the utility of female education in India. Vidya Sagar established forty girls' schools in Bengal between 1855 and 1858. He did not charge any fee from the students and provided them with books and stationery, free of cost. He also energized the mind of Bengal and emerged as a great upholder of women's cause.

Swami Dayanand Saraswati was the rare combination of intuition and intellect. Born in Kathiawad, Gujarat, in the year 1824, he became a great scholar of Sanskrit. At the age of fourteen, he began his quest after Truth, and struck by the transient nature of the material world, left home to become a Sanyasi. Swami Dayanand studied the Vedas and was initiated into Sanyasa by Swami Birjanand of Vrindaban. He toured the whole of India and propagated the Vedic teachings. For the revival of Aryan ideals and for the eradication of social evils, the foundation of Arya Samaj was laid at Bombay in 1875. He was a staunch advocate of female education and specially recommended the study of Vedas and other holy scriptures for women.

He told women to follow the example of Gargi and Maitreyi. He found favour with the idea that the educated women should take up the task of teachers. He opposed the early marriage of boys and girls both and condemned unequal marriages and the system of dowry. He also enumerated the abuses of polygamy and laid great stress on 'Brahmacharya'. He favoured the system of widow-remarriage, marriage by consent, and tried to revive the ancient practice of 'Swayamvara'. He pleaded that the widow's children should be given the right to inherit the property of their father in order to remove the problem of their upbringing. To execute his programme, the leaders of Arya Samaj opened a large number of Vedic girls' schools throughout northern India. By advocating the participation of those who had once been converted to other religions, Dayanand began the *Shuddhi* movement and procured their re-admission into Hindu society. Dayananda earned a great name by it.

The founders of Radhasoami faith allowed the women to join the daily Satsang. Huzur Maharaj Rai Salig Ram Bahadur was born in a reputed family of Agra. His father who was a famous lawyer, died early. His mother was an enlightened lady. She gave him an opportunity to avail the privilege of English education. A seeker of Truth, Huzur studied the Upanishads, Vedanta, the holy scriptures of Buddhism, Jainism, Vaishnavism, Shaivism and the literature of the medieval Saints and Sufis. He read the Quran and the Bible both. His inner quest continued for long and he desired to adopt the true spiritual guide and Master. He met his Guru Soami Ji Maharaj in 1858. On Huzur's insistence, Soamiji founded the Radhasoami faith in 1861. Huzur was the second guru of this sect and he worked from 1878 to 1898. He made it an all-India Movement. Absorbed as Huzur was in the spiritual ideals and values, he did not ignore social problems of the day. The deplorable condition of women attracted his sensitive mind, and through his fortnightly journal—*Prem-Patra*, he advocated the programme of women's emancipation and education.

He asserted that high status in learning or devotion to religion could not be attained by living in Purdah. According to him, Purdah and lack of education were the two main causes of women's degradation in society. He advocated equality of women with men on spiritual grounds. In face of bitter criticism by the orthodox section of society, Huzur Maharaj allowed women to attend regular *satsang* and perform *Guru-Bhakti*. He did not agree with the traditional belief that the husband is the virtual guru of his wife. He recommended that women should tread the path of spiritual life and practise Yoga. He pleaded for women's education and stressed the need of their compulsory primary training in domestic accounts and the study of scriptures. He was pained to see that women during his time were relegated to a low position and were confined in the household. He made a strong plea for their social and spiritual upliftment.

The third leader of Brahmo Samaj, Keshab Chandra Sen, was born in an enlightened family of Calcutta. He received his education at the Hindu College. In 1859, he staged a drama on widow re-marriage. He openly attacked the practice of Kulinism. He started 'Sangat Sabha' in 1860. Its members decided not to see public dances and to practise temperance. They resolved to impart to their womenfolk, the light of new knowledge so that they might become the true partners in life.

Keshab wanted to spread female education and he founded a number of Brahmo girls' schools. In 1863, he founded the 'Society of Theistic Friends' with the object of encouraging the habit of study among women who lived in the *Zenana*. Annual examinations were conducted for such women and the successful among them were awarded prizes. He started the publication of a monthly magazine *Bamabodhini* exclusively for women. In 1865 he inaugurated another branch for women known as Brahmika Samaj. It was an organization exclusively meant for women. Under the able leadership of Keshab the younger members of the Samaj protested against non- tolerance and denounced polygamy. An active spirit of social reform was shown by celebrating inter-caste marriages and removal of purdah for women. His campaign against early marriages facilitated the enactment of 'The Civil Marriage Act of 1872'.

M.G. Ranade was connected with more than twenty social organizations of Poona, and after 1881 his activities spread all over India. In 1887, he founded the Indian Social Conference. He was very liberal and he favoured widow re-marriage. He joined 'Widow Marriage Association' founded by Vishnu Shastri Pundit. He regarded the age for marriage as 12 and that of consummation as 16. He quoted in his support the verdict given in *Grihya Sutra* and firmly believed that a return to a respectable status of women was no innovation, but the return to the ancient glorious past of India.

Another renowned journalist, Behramji Malabari, was born in 1853 in a Parsi family. He was educated in a missionary school. He was inspired by the active humanitarianism of Christianity. With the fervour of a great social reformer, Malabari challenged the practice of early marriages and compulsory widowhood. Malabari said that "the sight of the mistreated widows, resounds into my brain. It is not merely that I know the miseries of widowhood, not merely that I feel for them but I become a widow myself for the time being." He founded a journal, *Indian Spectator*, for spreading his ideas of reform. He published two notes on 'Infant Marriages in India' and 'Enforced widowhood' in 1884. He argued that early marriage was sapping the vigour and vitality of the Hindu youth. He demanded from the government, aid and co-operation, to awaken the national conscience on the urgency of reforms. He laid stress upon the British officials to persuade the Government for enactment of social legislations. He also prepared the ground for the enactment of the Age of Consent Bill.

Born in 1858, Maharshi Karve was a well known Indian social reformer. He received his education at Elphinston College, Bombay and Fergusson College, Poona in 1891. As a Professor, he became a life member of the Deccan Education Society. A widower himself, Karve married a twenty three year old widow in 1893. In the same year, he revived the Widow Re-marriage Association of Poona. Karve had to face a lot of social ostracism and condemnation. In 1896, Karve established an association to collect funds for the Anath-Balika Ashram, which was an institution for female education. In 1907, he founded the Mahila Vidyalaya with the assistance of Deccan Education Society. He also laid the foundation of the Bombay Women's University in 1916. For training a body of selfless workers, he also established the 'Nishkam Karma Math'. His wife assisted him in his mission of giving an honourable place to the widows in society, of encouraging their re-marriages and enabling them to take respectable occupations in life after receiving proper education and training.

Rabindra Nath Tagore belonged to the famous Tagore family of Calcutta. His artistic nature found expression not only in his captivating poetry but also in his poetical prose. He enriched the Bengali language and heightened its musical quality. In 1855, he became the Secretary of the Adi Brahmo Samaj. By the devotional fervour of his songs and inspiring addresses to the members, he asserted his dedication to the ideals of Indian culture. In 1909, he started at Shanti Niketan, a school based on the pattern of ancient 'Tapovans'. In 1894, he advocated for communal unity as the basic principle of national progress. He formally inaugurated 'Visva Bharti' in 1929. Rabindra Nath Tagore glorified women in his literary compositions. He praised them for qualities of chastity, devotion and sincerity. He had faith in their inner strength and he exhorted upon them to rise to the occasion and play their legitimate role in society. Reviving the ancient ideals of Indian womanhood, he did not agree with the view that women were men's competitors. He considered them essentially as men's active partners in life. He admired the grace and sweet charm of women not as men's replica but as 'fellow pilgrims' in the journey of life.

Swami Vivekananda was born in a Kayastha family of Calcutta in 1869. He received English education. He was deeply interested in philosophy of Mill, Hume and Spencer. He was first attracted towards the Brahmo Samaj, but he could not get the desired peace and contentment there. In 1881, he met Ramkrishna at Dakshineshwar and was drawn towards him. He could reveal to him the light of Love and Truth. In 1897, he founded the Ramkrishna Mission.

Vivekananda wanted women to be emancipated from all restraints through education. He exhorted upon them to acquire the spirit of valour and heroism. He recommended such education as would make them useful members of society, self-dependent and self-reliant. He revived the ancient ideals regarding Indian women and believed in their innate virtues. He held that women possessed spiritual qualities and a regenerating power. He was convinced that if the status and position of women could be raised, India will surely be free and independent.

Vivekananda had a plan for establishing a 'Women's Math' where Brahmacharya would be the guideline of all activities. Attached to the Math, he wanted to set up a girls' school where celibate nuns would be trained to become teachers. He also felt that its branches should be established in different towns and villages in the country. As a rule, the guardians of the girls joining the female Math would not think of their marriage before the age of fifteen. Swami Vivekananda was against the custom of early marriage. He condemned it, because "it brought child bearing and early death of women, pregnancy of low vitality swelling the rank of beggars, widowhood and many other evils," He also helped Sister Nivedita to open a number of girls' schools in Bengal.

In south India, Pantulu and R. Venkata Ratnam Naidu were the members of the Theistic Samaj. Viresalingam was a staunch supporter of the women's cause. He devoted his life to the work of women's advancement through education. He, too, recommended marriage reforms. In 1878, he formed the Rajahmundry Social Reform Association and in 1891, he laid the foundation of Widow Re-marriage Association. He also established a Widow Home at Madras in 1902 which provided them boarding and education free of charge.

Deeply impressed by the personalities of Viresalingam and Pundit Shiv Nath Sastri, R.V. Raman became a member of Madras Brahmo Samaj. In 1905 he rose to be the Principal of Rajah College at Cocanada. He encouraged female education there. In 1925, as the Vice-Chancellor of Madras University, he made vigorous efforts for temperance and for stopping *Devdasi* system. He condemned the entire system of popular mythology and representations of established Hindu divinities on moral grounds which seemed to convey sexual licentiousness of what he called a sanctimonious sin. Later, his crusade against *Devdasi* system was taken up by the National Social Conference.

The ablest and most talented reformer, Gopal Krishna Gokhale was born in 1866. He was educated at Kolhapur and Bombay. He started his career as a teacher. He established the Servants of India Society in 1905 to carry on the work of social reform and service to the nation. Gokhale was deeply interested in the propagation of female education. He did not approve of the seclusion of women. He felt that, "combination of enforced ignorance and overacting in religion made them the willing victims of unjust and harmful customs."

In order to improve the women's lot, Gokhale suggested 'a wide diffusion of knowledge with all its solvent influences needed for the women of India.' He thought that education alone could "emancipate their minds from the degrading thraldom of defective ideas inherited through a long past." He believed that such an emancipation would "restore the women to their honoured position which they had, at one time, occupied in India." Gokhale laid stress upon proper handling of the problem of female education and warned against any hasty steps in the matter.

Born in 1869, Mohandas Karamchand Gandhi was

destined to play a great role in arousing political consciousness among the Indian masses. He also devoted his attention to the women's cause. Himself a sufferer, he considered it heresy and irreligious to give religious sanction to the custom of child marriage. He held that this practice was both fatal and immoral. Gandhiji deplored the treatment meted out to Hindu widows. He observed that "every widow had as much right to re-marry as every widower had. Voluntary widowhood may be considered a priceless boon in Hinduism, but enforced widowhood must not be imposed."

Gandhiji did not favour reforms by legislation. He considered it as an outside imposition. He believed that real reform could come firstly by the force of enlightened public opinion among Hindus and secondly by people's broad outlook on women's issues. He held that the custom of Purdah was a curse on women because chastity was neither a hot-house growth nor could it be super-imposed. He considered the system of dowry as a real drag on society. His call to the women to come out of their secluded apartments and work for the Indian freedom movement had a magical effect. He worked hard for bringing women on an equal footing with men. He considered that education was as necessary for women as for men. Through his journals, *Harijan* and *Young India*, he expressed his ideas about women's emancipation. He vehemently condemned the system of Devdasi and led a crusade against prostitution. He held men responsible for such types of women's degradation.

He wrote that, "Women are not the weaker sex. They are the very source of inspiration, and moral strength to men. Women are the embodiment of sacrifice, faith and patience." In fact, Gandhiji brought about a 'self-realization' among women. With his masterly pen and forceful tongue, he propagated the idea of women's progress and development. He had a burning desire to see them restored to their natural and rightful place in society. In his own programmes and institutions, he assigned equal place to them. Nothing delighted the reformers more than the success of women in any sphere of life. They could notice the stir of a new life among the women and prophesied that women were waiting to be organized.

The socio-religious reformers recommended female education and legal rights for them. They desired to elevate the women's lot. Many of them chalked out a positive and constructive programme of eradicating the social evils affecting the women. They established diverse institutions to bring about their socio-economic upliftment and progress. They opened Schools, Colleges, Widow Asylums and Vocational training Centres to give them ample opportunities of self-expression, self-reliance and self-development. They infused in them a new hope and aspirations by their speeches and writings.

Many of the reformers thought that national progress could not proceed in compartments, and political freedom could not fully thrive unless it was accompanied by economic prosperity and social equality. Many of them relied too much upon official interference and the enactment of social legislations as the remedy of all social evils. The reformers had to face strong opposition from the reactionaries in Hindu society. Often they had to bear insults, but they remained firm and true to their conviction. With undaunted courage and faith, they attempted to instal the women in the temple of social justice and fair treatment. They professed in favour of social reforms and strived hard to remove the spell of false traditions. They rightly advocated that true Hinduism meant a progressive and broad religious outlook along with a scientific approach to life.

It is indeed amazing that Indian men were the pioneers in this field and they made strong and sincere efforts for transforming the social scenario. They were indeed the great supporters of women's cause.

4. The Germination

When the male reformers took up their cause, Indian women followed close behind them and organized themselves in strong teams to launch a programme for their own resurgence. As a product of 19th century renaissance, some outstanding Indian women implanted the seeds of feminism in the country. These women not only stood up to challenge their age-long intellectual isolation but also boldly discard the obsolete customs and dead usages to which they had long remained a helpless victim. With their innate purity and moral force par excellence, they inaugurated the magnificent era of the women's movement in India. It appears that they felt an inner urge and a strange restlessness within their very souls to accomplish their own resurgence which necessitated the spirit of self-introspection and critical approach to the problems of their subordination and humiliation. Beneath the calm surface of their tortured life, a slow but steady upsurge soon became discernible. The women leaders effortlessly turned to India's glorious past and sought inspiration from the ideas and ideals of Indian womanhood during the Rigvedic period. With a rich heritage in the background, their long-awaited task began. They forged a pathway for the future generation to tread upon and they dared to walk through the solitary forest of gloom with bleeding feet. They were the women who wrote the first gold letters on the new horizon of India's future. They became the true path-finders and the lamp-posts to guide the future of the next generation of women.

The first among them was Pandita Ramabai who was born on 23rd April 1885 in the Gangamul forest—a plateau on one of the peaks of western Ghats in Mysore. Her father, Anant Shastri was a very learned and brave scholar and a devoted reformer. He successfully stormed the strong-hold of Shastric bigotry and orthodoxy and taught Sanskrit language and literature to his wife and daughter. He endured great persecution for his conviction that women had the same right to higher knowledge as the men had.

In Pandita's own words: "The people in the neighbourhood disapproved of him and threatened to put him out of caste. When they found that they could in no way prevail upon him to stop educating me and my mother, they went to a Dharma-Guru and brought the matter before him begging to enforce the law against my father, because he was a breaker of their sacred laws and customs. My father told to the Dharma-Guru, that female education is a Hindu custom. The Dharma Guru could not give a satisfactory answer."

Pandita imbibed the spirit of Protestantism from her parents while she gained scholarship and wisdom. Her learning and unmarried state evoked the curiosity and hostility among the people. She boldly faced all this, assimilating experience, watching the injustice and tyrannies with calm and critical eyes and unconsciously training and preparing herself for the great task she was destined to perform in near future. Her family had left the security of the forest home and taken to a nomadic life. Ramabai had the opportunity of touring many parts of the country, but she records with grief that "the pride of caste and superior learning, and vanity of life, prevented our stooping down to acquire some industry whereby we might have saved the precious lives of our parents." Pandita further writes: 'Ever since I remember anything, my father and mother were always travelling from one sacred place to another, staying in each place for some months, bathing in the sacred rivers and tanks, visiting temples, and reading the Puranas in temples of some convenient places."

Due to sorrow, helplessness and disgrace they faced, her father decided to drown himself, but her brother forced him to drop the idea. He decided to give up the caste pride and go to work to support his old parents. As her brother, Anant Shastri was weak and feeble, he died due to fever amidst the curse of poverty. The same year her mother also expired at Raichur. Pandita survived all the privations, tragedies and diseases to which her poverty-stricken life was exposed. A girl of sixteen, she emerged as an individual with a great mission in life. During her wanderings, she could gather enormous information and a vast experience. She was aware of the evils of caste, and the denial of education and salvation to women. She writes: "We travelled to different parts of India. We had a good opportunity of seeing the sufferings of Hindu women. We saw it not only in one part of India but it was the same in all the Presidencies as well as in Assam. It forced me to think about efforts to be made to improve the condition of women."

In 1878, she was examined in Sanskrit at Calcutta by three experts who were renowned scholars. They conferred on her the title of 'Saraswati'. She was later honoured by the title of 'Pandita'. Her fame began to spread far and wide. The intellectuals of Calcutta requested her to deliver a series of lectures on the emancipation of women. She herself records, "In the towns and cities, we often addressed large audience and urged upon them the need for education of women and children." She learnt Bengali and Hindi in order to converse with the people of different castes and provinces. Her lectures left a deep impact upon her listeners. In her own words, "I cannot describe all the sufferings of the terrible time. My brother and I survived and wandered about, still visiting sacred places bathing in rivers and worshipping the Gods and Goddesses.... We had fulfilled all the conditions laid down in the sacred books ... but the Gods were not pleased with us.... After years of fruitless service, we began to lose our faith in them." Miss Mary Lucia Fuller, one of the Pandita's biographers, writes, "Her speech was famous for its purity, its vigour, its freshness and range."

She attempted to awaken the women to abandon the evil practices of child-marriage, acquire regular education for themselves, and to do away with the wrongs meted out to them. During her earlier crusades, she campaigned with arguments based on the ancient scriptures. She realized that India was passing through a period of transition. She made her voice heard, breaking "the silence of a thousand years." She desired that Indian women must regain the position they once occupied during India's glorious past. She was well versed in the scriptures and could easily prove the sufferings of Indian women as the abuse of the time and a total misunderstanding of the spiritual sense contained in the religious texts. Her knowledge, eloquence, tact and inspiration were always supported by the Hindu scriptures and she won the hearts of all those who heard her.

Many have tried to trace western impact on Ramabai. In fact, her aching experiences of the terrible state of ignorance and degradation into which the Indian womanhood had sunk, her observation of the cases of cruelty, her father's struggle at the hands of the society, awakened her to the situation and urged upon her to work whole-heartedly for the upliftment of women. She urged the women not to fall victims to the evils inflicted upon them by an autocratic and orthodox priesthood. She made a close study of the lives of women in Bengal and was greatly moved by the sight of the cruel treatment meted out to them, which they silently suffered.

All these made her bitter and harsh and she decided to

interpret the socio-religious injunctions to open the eyes of the people. She could not reconcile with the ideas that women are sinful and they could not attain *Moksha*.

In her books and speeches, Ramabai fully explained the position of women as interpreted by the selfish purohits of Hinduism and struck a contrast between the position of Hindu women of her times and the one envisaged in the Hindu scriptures. In Bengal and Assam, her lectures on the emancipation of women revealed that the position of women in ancient India was really high, and that it was up to the women of her time to free themselves from the shackles imposed on them by the rules drawn up later in the name of their protection from the alien invaders.

After her brother's death, Pandita was left all alone in the world. The same year, she married a Kayastha gentleman Bipin Behari Das Medhavi who was a Brahmo. For marrying a Maharashtrian lady, Bipin Behari was excommunicated by his fellow caste-men and relatives. Ramabai lived happily with her husband in Silchar for nineteen months. Her husband died of cholera in 1882. She was left in this world with a new-born daughter. Ramabai again faced bitter criticism from the orthodox people, yet, she would not succumb to living a miserable life.

She herself recorded, "I became the subject to severe criticism. They objected to my inter-caste, inter-provincial marriage and also to my age."

In those days the society held the women responsible for their husband's death. 'The Karma of wife in previous birth causes the death of the husband'. The general belief at that time was this. Pandita consoled herself and left Assam, determi-ned to lead a life of extreme action. At first, she was condemned and criticized quite mercilessly for marrying out of her caste and then as an inauspicious widow whose karmas were responsible for her husband's death.

Despite all her sorrows and sufferings, she walked ahead

with her mission of social reform. She wished to have the *Shastras* interpreted in their true sense, letter, spirit and perspective and the women restored to their rightful status. Nothing could subdue her indomitable spirit. She proceeded to Madras and studied English language there. She visited Karachi and in the end, she came to Poona where M.G. Ranade and his wife welcomed her. She had many friends among the leaders of the social reform movement.

In order to eliminate the evil practices of child-marriage, to improve the condition of women and promote their education, Pandita started Mahila Samaj at Poona and a similar Samaj was established in Bombay.

These organizations were to serve as a nucleus to female agitation. She toured throughout the Bombay Presidency and established branch societies in different towns. She made eloquent appeal to the people in favour of the sublime cause of womens' emancipation. Pandita's magical personality attracted a large number of women to these organizations. She inspired many women workers to found similar institutions in Bengal where a reformer, Dwarkanath Ganguli took up the lead and published an appeal for the foundation of the Samitis. Despite the support of many reformers, Ramabai felt that she could not carry out the needed reforms. Her friends issued an appeal that, 'Such is the career of a lady who is doing so much for the unfortunate women of India, yet she can hardly achieve any success single handed. It is incumbent on men to set aside their apathy towards females, to give them the concessions they have a right to claim and to support them in their efforts towards progress. If they do not give a helping hand to the so-called feeble sex, a time will come when the members of their sex will form themselves into a strong community, and challenge them in open war. It is hoped that our enlightened brethren in different parts of India will lend them support towards the establishment of branch Associations and induce their female relatives to join the Society. It is hoped that the National Indian Association will give its cordial support to their movement." Pandita quite realized that she should have sufficient money and support for her programmes which the Indians did not extend whole-heartedly. She welcomed the Education Commission in the Town Hall, Poona, on 5th September 1882 which came to India to investigate the prospects of women's eduction. Dr. W.W. Hunter, the President of the Commission, highly respected Pandita and stressed that her evidence was of great importance. She suggested to the Commission that the charge of female schools should be given to the female teachers, that the government should take prompt action to check oppression and cruel treatment to women and pursue a policy of equal justice and make provision for the study of medicine by the Indian women to save the lives of multitudes. In one of her lectures she said that "Men look on women as chattels. We shall make every effort to deliver ourselves out from this situation."

Her appearance before the Hunter Commission and her wide lecture programmes attracted the attention of the Indian people. Her bold suggestions for female education were widely applauded. Her plea for medical aid drew the attention of queen Victoria who took personal interest in the matter. The National Association for supplying Female Medical Aid to the women of India was inaugurated by Lady Dufferin in 1885. Ramabai summarized these needs and placed them before the government as back as 1882. Her efforts brought positive results.

Pandita decided to go to England to learn more about women's education and to receive a good training for her work. The excommunication for crossing the sea could not detract her from the path she had chosen. She had failed in her project to start a Widow's Home. She then decided to study medicine and be of tremendous help to the women of the country.

A daily newspaper of Bombay reported, 'All the natives had grown to be proud of her. The more advanced natives saw in what she taught, the possibilities of a regenerated society and religion.'

Pandita wrote a book *Stree Dharma Neeti* and with the money collected from the sale of the book, she was able to purchase a part of her passage abroad. The book was meant for guiding the women to live a life of enlightenment instead of being blind slaves to tradition.

She sailed for England on 20th April, 1883, and lived there with the sisters of Wantage Mission. In England she embraced Christianity which gave solace to her. At Cheltenham College, she found a life long friend in Miss Beale, a pioneer British educationist. There, she improved her knowledge of English and studied Mathematics, Natural Sciences and other allied subjects. Pandita wrote that, "the human heart will break into thousand pieces at the very thought of the shameful position in which the women are placed." Ramabai thus germinated the seeds of restlessness among Indian women. "Once Ramabai set the ball rolling, a great deal of freedom of speech and writing followed over the years." It is interesting to note that stress was laid by the Indian reformers on Pandita's learning and enlightenment.

For further studies, she sailed for USA in 1886. From there she got the idea of founding schools in India which would combine the "training of the hand with that of the head." She also felt the great need in India for kindergarten schools. She made many friends from among the missionaries, educationists, doctors and teachers. She left the course of Medicine on account of hard hearing and joined Kindergarten training school for a year. From July 1886 onwards she translated the approved text-books in Marathi. In order to cover the cost of publication of these books, she wrote *The High Caste Hindu Woman*, which sold like hot cakes.

In USA, she delivered her first public lecture in Philadelphia and held the audience spell-bound with her eloquence and impassioned plea for the social amelioration of women. Pandita wrote in 1886, "I am deeply impressed by and interested in the work of western women, who seem to have one common aim namely, the good of their fellow-beings. It is my dream, some day to tell my country women in their own language this wonderful story, in the hope, that the recital may awaken in their hearts a desire to do likewise." She delivered the message that, "Educate the high caste child widows, for, I solemnly believe that this hated and despised class of women, if educated and enlightened, will redeem India." A Ramabai Association was started on 28th May, 1887 in Boston. Her endurance was marvellous even in the eyes of Americans. She travelled to different parts of America and Canada, lecturing, forming groups, studying educational methods and completely preparing herself for the new task ahead. When Ramabai was assured of an income to support fifty pupils for ten years, she decided to return home and start her experiments in India. During her return voyage, she stayed in Japan for thirteen days. She was invited by the Women's Christian Temperance Union of Tokyo. She addressed eight meetings there. She landed in Calcutta on February 1889. From there she went straight to Poona. She recorded that "Almost all the time of my sojourn in the foreign countries, I was constantly busy studying the people, their language and customs. It was in America that my efforts showed signs of fruit," ... "I addressed, while touring, three hundred meetings and the foreign people were moved with pity. I travelled over 30,000 miles and raised Rs.60,000 for this mission. Besides this, they have further assured a generous grant of Rs. 15,000 per annum for a period of ten years. A regular organization has been duly established for this purpose at Boston with sixty four sub-branches all over the country."

Ramabai laid the foundation of Sharda Sadan and spent her most fruitful active years in social work. She became an outstanding personality both in the Indian National Congress circle and in the meetings of Indian Social Conference. She addressed the Indian National Congress meeting held at Bombay as a representative of Arya Samaj and said: "It is not strange, my countrymen, that my voice is small, for you have never given a woman the chance to make her voice strong."

In 1889, she wrote another book *The Peoples of the United States*. She frankly criticized American customs and manners and laid stress upon the capacity of women to overcome superstitious and reactionary customs and build a world of education, love and good citizenship. In 1890, she shifted to Sharda Sadan, Poona. She faced bitter criticism of the reformers, when two of the girls living with her embraced Christianity. The members of the Advisory Board resigned in 1893, but she firmly dealt with the situation and carried on her work, undaunted and unaffected. She was a great patriot and a daring lady, who may rightly be called a tradition-breaker. Her spirit of reform evoked high appreciation among her friends and bitter criticism of the opponents. When the Sadan was formally opened in Poona in 1892, she desired it to become a loving home for the women in problems.

She said: "My Hindu brethren thought I was Christianizing the girls ... they wanted to pull our school down and raise another school on its ruins, but I am glad to say that the foundations of this school have not been set on sand."

Pandita Ramabai had to face a great crisis, when the matron was found exercising a bad influence over the women of Sharda Sadan. She removed the matron-who thereafter joined the great army of her opponents in the city and spread all sorts of scandals. The Advisory Board took exception to her Christian teachings and withdrew about twenty-five girls from Sharda Sadan. Anonymous letters threatening her and papers full of abuses were the rewards that she received. The Ramabai Association in America also reprimanded her for breaking the strict secular atmosphere. Even her friends accused and abandoned her. Ramabai, great as she was, would neither apologize nor vindicate herself. She later wrote, "Our efforts to educate the widows and help other women are far from being liked. The storm raised against our school by some people has somewhat subsided, but the spirit of opposition is still alive. Some are carried away so far by their prejudices that they think that it is a sin to support and educate widows."

The number of women rose to forty nine in Sharda Sadan. Her influence increased and she was greatly respected for her motherly love and wisdom. The same year she visited many parts of India in order to investigate the condition of widows. She had heard that in the temples the priests were using widows for immoral traffic and increasing the number of temple prostitutes. In the disguise of a religious beggar woman, she went to Vrindaban. She lived there for fifteen days and could convince seven widows to come with her to Poona, but they were locked up by the priests. She could rescue only one against threat to her life. During the famine of 1897, she started relief work. Due to her strenuous activities in the camp the rescue of about sixty women became possible. Later, she noted that "Being dressed as a religious beggar, and caring little what people said or what might happen to me, I went round to all the houses of the town with open eyes to see the condition of the widows. I saw hundreds and hundreds of them ... hundreds I might say thousands, of widows young and old who came there every year and fell into the snares of the priests.... When they got an order and did not go to please the men, they were turned out of the house to care for themselves as best they can ... the sin and misery and heartless cruelty of men to these women are beyond all description."

Ramabai travelled in the area of famine under great risks and dangers from dacoits and wild animals. She carried on her work undaunted. She also took up the work of developing a hundred acres of land into a farm at Kedagaon. By 1900, she had firmly established the Mukti Sadan where she started a Normal School. She opened a Boy's Orphanage and the Kripa Sadan—a refuge for the fallen. Mukti Sadan was a vast settlement of a purely philanthropic character.

She realized that it was essential for women to work. She popularized professions of nursing, teaching and work in industries among the middle class women and trained countless women of lower classes for other jobs that suited them. The gallant lady triumphed in her struggle against conservatives and reactionaries. Helen Dyer who visited Sharda Sadan in 1892, noticed that the girls loved Ramabai and followed her after school hours like bees.

Taking inspiration from Ramabai, many humanitarian institutions came up in the country. D.K. Karve owed the idea of Widow's Home to the Pandita. Many of the widow asylums were opened in Madras and Bengal. Max Muller assessed her by asserting that, "She is certainly the most courageous woman, not to be turned away from her purpose by any misfortune or threat. Far sighted as she was, she planned the future after every setback with a fresh zeal and renewed faith in God. Despite her absorption in her own institutions, she continued to take a lively interest in the welfare of the people of Poona. She did outstanding services during the plague epidemic."

She made bold statements criticizing the authorities and objected to the manner in which women were treated by the doctors. She planned various forms of work for independent economic existence of the women who lived with her.

Her daughter, Manorama, who enthusiastically worked for her mother's cause, died in 1921. This irreparable loss and the excessive work weakened the physical health of Pandita.

Still she worked during the day and prayed at night. In 1922, Ramabai passed away from this world. The Hindus and Christians mourned alike, the loss of the great daughter of India. Mrs. Sarojini Naidu described her at a meeting in Bombay in 1922 as the first Christian to be enrolled in the calendar of Hindu Saints. She worked and died for the women's cause. She was a great woman, a great reformer, and above all a great pathfinder who germinated the seeds of a Women's Movement in India.

Another great luminary of the women's movement was Ramabai Ranade. She was born in 1862 in an orthodox Maharashtra family and was married to Mahadev Govind Ranade at the age of eleven in 1873. Uneducated and young as she was, she experienced a sense of awe in the presence of her enlightened husband, whose fame as a renowned scholar and an active reformer had spread far and wide. M.G. Ranade was older to her by twentyone years. He was a great protagonist of female education and in spite of great opposition at home, he started imparting English education to his girl-wife. In the traditional joint family set up, Ramabai Ranade had to face great hurdles for her aspirations to be educated. After the exacting household duties, she devoted her free time to her studies. She made astonishing progress and amazed her husband by her sharp intellect.

Her biographer says that, "The bitter taunts she heard downstairs, could not damp the joy she felt as she sat upstairs and recited Sanskrit shlokas or read Meadow Taylor's thrilling Tara or Sita aloud to the Judge. What did it matter if, after a joyous meeting at one of Pandita Ramabai's lectures, on coming home, she was abused and not allowed to help in the kitchen work with the women of the family, until she had a bath of purification! Even the water for the bath had to be drawn from a well outside, not from the fountain within the sacred place of their home."

Her public life started in 1878, when she was only sixteen.

She invited women belonging to different towns for the celebration of Haldi-Kumkum. The object behind it was to impress on the need of female education in the exclusive gathering of women. She joined the Arya Mahila Samaj in 1881 and became its enthusiastic worker. She herself visited the *zenana* of many houses in Bombay and Poona, and persuaded the ladies to join the Samaj. She worked untiringly for the propagation of female education and emerged forth as the "typical daughter of her land—Maharashtra. She was simple, hard-working, hard-headed, soft-hearted, practical, idealistic, patriotic, parochial, shy, brave, conservative, pioneering—a paradox of good qualities but supremely a servant of her sisters with a life dedicated to their advancement." The objectives with which she started the work of women's emancipation were the following:

1. Through regular classes, to impart religious, literary, scientific, medical and industrial knowledge to women.
2. In addition to these classes, to create interest among women for library work, excursions, etc.
3. To prepare women for service, both at home and in the country at large.
4. To promote unity and fellowship amongst the women of India.
5. To work towards the general welfare of women.
6. To adopt such measures as may be necessary to open institutions for the promotion of these objectives and ideals.

In 1881, very few women attended the Arya Mahila Samaj. A small number of girls joined the High School for Indian Girls School at Poona in 1884, but they had to go in closed carriages escorted by elderly members of their families. It was the time when the women wearing footwear or carrying umbrella were the objects of general derision.

Ramabai Ranade had to carry her work in an orthodox and conservative setting.

Justice Ranade died in 1901 after a short illness. After a year of overwhelming grief, she composed herself and resolved to dedicate her life to the service of humanity in general and the uplift of women in particular. The twenty seven years of companionship with her husband had well prepared her for the onerous task that she took up. She emerged as a simple and unassuming leader of many unfortunate and under-privileged women. Service and sacrifice were the motto of her life. She threw herself whole-heartedly into the campaign for women's suffrage. She visited the prisons and comforted the women prisoners. She read aloud to them Tukaram's Abhangs (hymns) which she translated in simple Marathi.

From 1893 onwards, she showed great organizational capacity as President of Arya Mahila Samaj. With the help of some other ladies, she founded in another part of Bombay, the Hindu Ladies Social and Literary Club in order to train the women by teaching in regular classes and institutions. Her dream of the 'Home of Service' became a reality when through her marvellous plans, the Seva-Sadan grew into a big institution with its branches spread all over the Presidency of Bombay. Her big achievement was the foundation of Seva Sadan Nursing and Medical Association. Under her inspiration, the high caste Hindu women and widows volunteered for Nursing and Midwifery.

Ramabai Ranade organized free classes to educate married women and widows. She began training them in sewing, knitting and embroidery, and also arranged weekly lectures on subjects of general interest and first aid. She received for the Seva Sadan financial assistance from well to do ladies belonging to different communities and religions. In 1903, she became a member of the Lady Dufferin Fund Committee. Eminent persons like R.G. Bhandarkar, Annie

Besant, Mahatma Gandhi, Rabindra Nath Tagore and prominent visitors from abroad visited the Seva Sadan and paid their regards to her.

With zeal and optimism, she seized every opportunity to serve the needy and the poor. She paid regular visits to the public hospitals at Poona, and distributed fruits and books to the indoor patients. She used to visit the Boys' Reformatory School at Poona and Yervada Central Prison. She helped the Poona Municipality by undertaking the care of women pilgrims and children in the annual fair of Alandi.

In 1910, during the devastating fire at Salumbra in Poona district, Ramabai Ranade presided over the Relief Committee and did a pioneering work of service by comforting the injured and helping them. She led a group of enthusiastic workers from Seva Sadan who distributed foodgrains, clothes and medicines to the affected people.

Ramabai Ranade collected and published the lectures of Justice M.G. Ranade in 1902. Later in 1910, she published her 'Reminiscences' which was translated into many other Indian languages. Between the years 1920 and 1924, as a member of the Government Text Book Committee, she reviewed hundreds of books specially concerned with women and children. In 1904, while presiding over the first session of Bharat Mahila Parishad, she laid great stress on the need for female education. She emphasized the spirit of changing time which necessitated increased participation of women in philanthropic, social and educational training. She presided over the meeting of Bharat Mahila Parishad on three more occasions between 1907 and 1920.

In 1914, Ramabai Ranade took a prominent part in the public protest against the imperialistic policies towards Indians in South Africa. She led an agitation for free and compulsory primary education for girls in 1920. She also took a leading part in the women's suffrage movement. Between 1919 and 1922 she organized large scale meetings, made speeches and wrote articles in support of the movement. In the Bombay Legislative Council, the mention of her very name turned the tide and later the women got the right to vote.

After a short illness she left her mortal frame in the year 1924. Thousands of men, women and children mourned her sad demise.

The light of love which she lit remained illuminating in the hearts of the devoted workers of Seva Sadan. They continued striving for the sublime cause on the model set by the great lady. It is an established fact of history that Ramabai Ranade was a social reformer of repute and a great initiator of the Indian women's movement. Not only did she made the Indian women conscious of their socio-political rights but she undertook great constructive projects which ultimately led to the betterment and upliftment of women in India. She taught the women to conserve what was excellent in the indigenous culture and also to assimilate that which was the best in the culture of the west. Her dedication and service are the prized possessions of Indian Womanhood today.

There were other women who lined like light-houses for the women sailing in the rocky path of self-regeneration, independence and excellence.

Born in 1865 at Poona, Anandi Bai (Yamuna) was one of them. She was a woman of courage and enterprise. Her father, Ganpatrao Amriteshwar Joshi was a wealthy landlord. Her mother, Gangabai Joshi was an intelligent lady. Like Ramabai, Anandi Bai also belonged to a Maharashtrian Chitpavan Brahmin family. From her childhood, Anandibai showed a 'bright and intelligent disposition'. She inherited from her father an iconoclastic zeal and she rebelled against the traditional ritualism. She was married at the age of nine to Gopal Vinayak Joshi—a clerk in the Postal Department. He began teaching his young wife. Gopal Vinayak was transferred first to Kolhapur and then to Bombay. Finally he was promoted as Post Master of Cutch. Anandibai, thus got an opportunity to visit different places and study the social condition of women. She sharply reacted against their extremely backward condition.

In 1878, her only child was born, who lived only for a few days. She was deeply shocked, and was convinced that with proper medical treatment, the child would have survived. She then realized the urgent necessity of women doctors in India. She herself decided to study medicine. She expressed her desire to go to America to which her husband agreed. He wrote a letter to an American editor for assistance. The editor did not promise any help but he published the letter in his magazine. Mrs. B.F. Carpenter, an American lady, who longed to help India, went through the letter in the magazine. She immediately wrote to Anandibai and both became friends. Anandibai was assured of all help and co-operation from her. So she sailed for America in 1883 all alone, where Mrs. Mary Carpenter received her with great warmth. She later wrote about Anandibai, "I have been drawn into close connection with one, whose noble character and high purpose of life attracts all men and women."

Anandibai possessed a great zeal to serve her country and ameliorate the deplorable condition of the health of Indian women. She started her studies at the Women's Medical College, Philadelphia. She worked hard, though the cold climate and strenuous work began to tell upon her health. Even in the foreign land, she preserved her own cultural values. She cooked her own food in her room.

In March 1886, she graduated. She appeared at the final tests and came out successful. It was a great occasion. Many friends, admirers and her husband gathered round her. Pandita Ramabai also reached to congratulate her.

Anandibai wanted to continue her studies further. But due to her failing health, she was compelled to return to India. She accepted the post of Resident Physician in the Women's

Ward of the New Albert Eduard Hospital at Kolhapur. Her health deteriorated. She contracted tuberculosis and passed away.

There were many other distinguished women, who pioneered the cause of female education and contributed to the growth and development of women's movement in India.

Francina Sorabjee was a great advocate of female education. She decided to establish Girls' schools in the western parts of India. Francina thought that unity was the first and foremost need of the country. As such, she envisaged a plan to organize schools where unity and integrity might be fostered easily. She founded three large schools at Poona, one for Marathi children, one for Muslim girls and the other for the training of teachers. In 1872, the Teachers' Training School founded by her became famous as the only school of its kind.

A brilliant scholar, Annie Jagannadhan went to Edinburgh in 1888. She joined the newly started Edinburgh School of Medicine for Women. In 1892, after passing the examination with triple qualification of the Scottish College, she returned to India. The same year, she took up the post of House surgeon at the Cama Hospital in Bombay. Her death in 1894 was a rude shock to the enlightened Indian women who expected from the young doctor useful service for the women of India.

Rakmabai, a victim of Indian traditionalism, rebelled against it and decided to study medicine. She refused to live with her husband and faced bitter criticism from the society. Her husband filed a suit against her. She was ordered six month's imprisonment if she did not agree to live with him.

Brought to a compromise by which a big sum of money was paid to her husband. She preferred punishment than to live with her husband. According to Hindu Law, Rakmabai could never marry again. However, she sailed for England where she studied medicine in London University. She took up the degree of Doctor of Medicine in 1895. She, then, returned to India and till 1929 when she retired, she remained in charge of Women's Hospital, Rajkot. In her free time, she worked for the women's cause and gave impetus to the programmes of women's movement.

These were the great women of the 19th century India, who in the face of mighty opposition, bravely carried on the work of women's emancipation. It is beyond doubt that they succeeded in their great mission. They gave worthy guidance and right direction to the women's movement in its very wake. All of them laid emphasis on the urgent need of female education in the country. They constantly preached for raising the socio-economic status of women. Certainly they achieved glory and greatness with their rare qualities of head and heart.

These women became the source of inspiration and a beacon light for the later leaders of the Indian feminist movement. It is beyond doubt that they inaugurated an era of great awakening among Indian womanhood. They definitely outlined the path of the Women's Movement in India. With the advent of the twentieth century, the country witnessed a rare awakening among the urban women of India, who founded the All India Women's Conference and many other organizations with genuine programmes of women's progress and prosperity.

5. The Horizon Expands

In the twentieth century, the horizon of women's movement in India began to expand rapidly. More consolidated and definite efforts were made in the field of women's education, health, social status and legal security. The demand for equal status in society and equal political rights found a general expression through various institutions of women. The trend towards feminism suddenly found a powerful expression and flowered in the country, as if it was some long awaited yet hidden impetus that pushed the movement. Women assumed the leadership and attempted to expand the horizon of women's world which indeed grew with remarkable vigour and audacity.

Besides the work of the socio-religious reformers and the concerted efforts of the early women pioneers, there were many other factors responsible for the rapid spread of awakening among Indian women. The women, who acquired the novel force of western liberalism, attempted to fulfil an inner urge for freedom and self-development. They were keen for social and political service of motherland. Raj Kumari Amrit Kaur gave expression to the instinctive desire of women to rise to the full liberty of soul. Many other enlightened women leaders aspired to give the message of their fullest development as human beings. To serve whole-heartedly and to give without stint was the burning passion of such women and an essential part of the development of free and awakened women. They began a battle against apathy, prejudices and ignorance. There was within them a passion for reform and change for betterment. In fact, the women gathered courage and confidence to clearly express themselves. They were no longer willing to submit to the standards, whether legal, political or ethical, which had been set for them by men through the ages. They had zealously become aware that such standards had been allowed to imply the complete subordination or even degradation of all classes of women just for being a woman. To quote Raj Kumari Amrit Kaur, ... "We are aware of the necessity of finding and being judged by our own standards as free human beings. We are determined to face the facts of life, to fight the battle of our sex and for this to take all risks...."

The emphasis on female education by the Christian missionaries, by the indigenous reformers and by the women leaders themselves, ultimately became the most potent factor in spreading the spirit of self-consciousness among them. Almost all the women's organizations echoed the demand for universal, free and compulsory education and also ample facilities for higher and technical education for women. With the spread of English education among men, the ideal of an enlightened home could not be achieved without equal education for life-partners. As a result many of the educated men started educating the female members of the family in the house.

They wished to impress upon the necessity of women's participation in the social life, and they tried to remove the disparity at home. Referring to this impact which education made on the status of women O'Malley remarks, "It was like a spiritual revolution profoundly affecting the foundations of society, of the home, and of the relationship of men and women." The middle class people inevitably attempted to follow the life style of upper class educated women who in imitation of western women, participated in social and intellectual gatherings outside even their homes. The men became keen to educate their wives and daughters so as to enable them to participate in socio-intellectual activities. Education began to make its way in the secluded apartments of the 'zenana' and infuse a new spirit of awakening in the so far "cabined, cribbed and confined" life of the Indian females.

Besides education, the attempt on the part of some women to cast off their shy temperament and adopt certain useful professions like nursing, teaching and other public services, inaugurated an era of socio-economic liberty for the womenfolk. Gradually, the Indian people became accustomed to see women undertaking various jobs. The changing pattern of socio-economic life, ultimately led to a remarkable awakening among the women. From the state of parasitic existence, they emerged as individuals socially useful and economically important.

The speed with which the country became united and integrated under British imperialist rule, dazzled everyone. The women, too, could not escape the impact of the political and administrative set up of the alien rule. Margaret Cousins writes, "In the sphere of womanhood and its rapid evolution in the last 50 years, the emergence of a consciously restored unity of India had begun from the political areas." She delivered a memorable series of public lectures in Madras entitled, 'Wake up, India', which resonated throughout the country as a clarion call to the people to work out their own salvation. She exhorted upon the Indians to free their girls from illiteracy and the custom of child-marriage, to free the outcastes from all religious sanctions. She asked the people to think about their degradation, slavery and suffering.

Cousins asserted that there should be freedom for men as well as for women. When Annie Besant formed the Home Rule League, there undoubtedly began an accentuation of the ideal of unity in India, and women of different provinces got together to exchange their views on the vital national issues. Even earlier, when the Indian National Congress was established in 1885, it had welcomed and included women members to its fold in 1900. It provided a congenial setting for the members of different geographical and linguistic areas to know one another personally, to participate in deliberations useful for the whole country and to imbibe the 'all-Indian' character of its sessions. It cannot, therefore, be denied that the women's movement, which was earlier expressing itself through individual efforts and aspirations, now received an increased impetus from the Indian National Congress and its collective and all-embracing programmes.

When Mahatma Gandhi entered the political scene, and the Indian women in large numbers came from different places and even from schools and colleges to participate in the national movement, feminism got a great momentum. It was on Gandhiji's call that women, from all over India, came forward, defying all social taboos, sacrificing physical comforts, and denying the validity of all restrictions which had been enforced upon them. They were ready to take up every kind of work connected with the political struggle. His unique contribution was to facilitate the awakening of the immense womanhood of India. It was indeed a new call to women's untapped energy to join the national struggle. He was determined to utilize their strength most advantageously for the progress of the national movement. A passionate believer in the principle of equality of women, he was doubtful in the beginning whether the women of India who were for long shut up in seclusion could shoulder the active leadership of a movement which called for so much physical suffering. When the programmes of Indian National Congress began under his leadership, he was satisfied to note that women had all the potential to bear difficulties and hard life. He said that, "the women of India should have as much honour in winning swaraj as men. Probably in this peaceful struggle, women could outdistance men by many a mile ... the Government of Bengal has dragged women into the line of fire and I hope that women all over India will take up the challenge and organize themselves to share the hardships along with men."

K.M. Panikkar later noted that the women, "belonging both to towns and villages were everywhere at the forefront. Indian women who had seemed to be deeply entrenched in 'the fortress of inviolable privilege and ignorance,' abandoned their traditional seclusion with dramatic suddenness." They gathered courage to combat their social degradation, and demanded an equal status in society. They suddenly appeared on the political scene and showed their potential power and capacity to shape the national destiny. With alacrity, they passed from apathetic indifference to eager appreciation of their responsibility, to march ahead and adopt a constructive programme of bringing the feminist movement to maturity and fruition.

The movement that the Indian women conducted for political suffrage in 1917 gave the true evidence of their courage and self consciousness. O'Malley rightly says that "There is a breath-taking abruptness about the entry of Indian women into political life. One moment they were not there, the next they fully arrived into the forefront." He further adds that, "'Phenomenal' is the adjective in the commonest use to describe their progress. They became conscious of the claims of national life almost over-night. In Bombay, for instance, women who did not know their way along the main streets, and had never seen the sea, formed themselves into a band of Desh Sevikas and walked in processions."

About fourteen women waited on Chelmsford, the Viceroy and Montague, the Secretary of State for India, in Madras City on 18th December 1917. These women came from different parts of India, and their Memorandum contained the demands of Indian women for better and increased services and the same franchise rights as was to be extended to men. The Memorandum itself marked a distinct milestone in the history of women's movement. It demanded the abolition of the disqualification on grounds of sex in the administrative sphere and in Local Government and under Legislative franchise Rules.

It was Margaret Cousins who actually organized the Deputation of women. She writes, "As the organizer of the Deputation, I happen to know that woman suffrage was not mooted when I first applied for permission to wait on the great men. The draft spoke only of education and social reforms, but the Secretary wrote that deputations would be received only on political subjects. I then circulated a couple of extra sentences about 'political rights' or rather opportunities for political service."

In her own heart she thought that it would be a century before Indian women would understand, or be interested in political matters. She confessed that she entirely underrated them. While working with Indian women leaders and watching their work, she could realize that Indian women were amongst the most intelligent in the world. Mrs. Besant, Mrs. Sarojini Naidu, Mrs. Herabai Tata and Miss Mithan Tata were the delegates who were so convincing in their arguments that the Parliament decided to consider, "Votes for Indian Women", a domestic subject which Indian Provincial Legislatures should settle for themselves, the official Government members being left free to vote as they liked."

The legislatures of different provinces, one after another, enfranchised the women on the same footing as men. Women grasped its importance at once and eagerly demanded a vote for every adult women. The British women had to struggle hard for suffrage rights. When the British Parliament considered the matter of Indian women, it was not expected that Indians would so easily take such a revolutionary step in spite of their rigid and conservative approach towards women. The Indian women were placed on the electoral rolls in Madras and Bombay in 1921, United Provinces in 1923, The Central Provinces, Punjab and Bengal in 1926. "With one hand the Indian women joined the passive resistance and with the other the vote." In fact by 1929, the Electoral Vote was one of the links making Indian womanhood a vital unit in the life of the country.

From around the year 1917, another subject came up to infuse an all India unity amongst women, namely the Health Services. The organization of All India Maternity and Child Welfare Association carried on the work of creating a wide interest in the welfare of the mother and the child both. Child Welfare Centres and pre-natal Clinics were opened. The Lady Reading Health Centre and All India Central Conference were opened at Delhi in 1927. The Girls' Guide movement also fostered unity among girls and loosened the bonds of conservatism by making them alive to their independent role and proving the usefulness of a disciplined life. In different provinces women formed organizations for social service, spread of education and for economic and religious purposes.

The linking process began by founding the All India Women's Conference in 1926. This organization siphoned all the scattered energies into a compact unit where the women could find the forum for expressing their grievances and putting their demands as well as for demonstrating their collective strength.

Most of the rural women worked hard in the fields and pastures and often served in the different village industries. When Gandhiji took up the lead in the national struggle, these rural women experienced the wave of a new awakening. The spark of political awakening among the rural masses of India was begun by Gandhiji.

Referring to the awakening among rural women, Margaret Cousins says, "The future of these millions of women would have caused one to despair, but for the marvellous awakening that the Indian National Congress has brought about, through Mahatma Gandhi's leadership of the masses in the villages." Gandhiji's call made its first impact in 1921, chiefly in towns, but since 1929 the spirit of patriotism, the awareness to political subjection and the demand for national freedom spread like a wild fire and caught the passions also of innocent village women-folk. In 1928, the price of salt was unjustly raised by the British and the women rebelled. When the Salt Satyagraha protest March was launched by Gandhiji, the most illiterate and conservative women became interested in joining him. Cousins further writes, "When a call for volunteers for Satyagraha action came, and men from the village responded, women who understood through their emotions and through their intuition, responded and nearly 5,000 of them suffered imprisonment, while hundreds of thousands—nay, millions of them were co-sufferers with men in the repressions of 1929 and 1933." In fact a new life swept through the villages and it vivified the women as much as the men. Their help was recognized and valued. All these women felt a new sense of power which they enjoyed for the first time. The struggle for freedom widened the interests of the women and opened new vistas before them. They attended the Congress meetings and after the men had been sent to jails, they took up their place and stood in the forefront with great enthusiasm and self-confidence. The enthusiasm indeed became infectious and a number of them cheerfully joined the band of Desh Sevikas permanently. Men, of course, were astonished at their courage and capacity to suffer patiently. They began to revise their opinion about women and see them in a completely new perspective. Instead of being shy of one another, they became help-mates and colleagues. The women felt elated and elevated when they were transformed into liberated souls—through expansion into something greater than merely individuals.

The trends of their awakening were visible among such rural women also as did not come out to participate in the national movement. While busy in their daily routine, they used to sing songs about the national heroes and the activities of the Congress. The folk songs of that period reflect the aspirations of women towards freedom and self-development. They glorified the ideal of patriotism and expressed their pious wish to see the tricoloured flag flying aloft in the country.

The credit for infusing such an awakening among Indian women must go to the standard bearers who by single minded purpose, devotion to duty and dedication to the sublime cause delivered the Indian women of their social fetters and led them to an honoured position in society. Dr. Annie Besant devoted her life to the cause of Indian freedom movement. She was married in 1867 to Frank Besant. The marriage did not last long. After seeking divorce from her husband, Mrs. Besant worked in various professions as cook, nurse, and journalist. She gave her first speech at London demanding equality for women in all spheres. She was a rank reformer, and a free thinker. She desired "to spread liberty and true thought among men, to wage war against bigotry and superstition and to make the world freer and better." She joined the Theosophical Society. After the death of Madam Blavatsky in 1892, she came to be the top rank leader. She regarded India as her true home. In 1893, she migrated to India to take up her cherished work in this country.

She once proclaimed, "I would urge on those who believe in women's natural inferiority, why in the name of common-sense, are you too terribly afraid of putting your theory to the proof."

She toured the entire country to acquaint herself with its

religion, philosophy, social manners and customs. She then delivered lectures on the great cultural heritage of India. She appealed to the Indians to revive their glorious past in the socio-religious life of the country and regain political freedom. She opened schools and colleges for "improving the morals of Hindu students and for engendering a love for Aryan simplicity and Aryan spirituality." She raised her voice against untouchability and was a great champion of female education. She held that girls must be educated as wives and mothers, not as the rival or competitors of men in all forms of outside and public employment. In 1906, she organized, within the Theosophical Society, the League for Social Service, and called the members as the 'Sons of India' and the 'Daughters of India'. She also established an organization known as the 'Theosophical Stalwarts' which later came to be known as 'Brothers of Service'. Her reputation as a great reformer and educationist soon spread far and wide. She was equally interested in the country's freedom and pleaded for the grant of Home Rule to Indians. With her firm determination and enthusiastic zeal, she carried on an energetic propaganda throughout India, moving on the wings of time and electrifying the people by an appeal to their emotions. She pointed out that the British rule was responsible for the economic exploitation of India. She started an all-embracing movement for the progress and development of India. According to her, India was a tremendous reservoir of man-power, far greater than America, and India under Home rule would be an asset to the Empire in the struggle against German militarism. For Annie Besant, it was imperative to grant freedom to India for the self-respect and dignity of such people who were in ancient age, the top-most civilization of the world.

Mrs. Besant gave a new turn to the women's programmes in India, when she favoured the idea of 'Vote for women', and served on the Delegation to the Secretary of State for

India. She was elected the President of the Indian National Congress in 1917. Under her Presidentship, the Congress expressed the opinion that the "same tests be applied to women as to men in regard to franchise and the eligibility to all elective bodies concerned with local government and education."

As the first woman President of the Congress, Mrs. Besant enhanced the prestige of Indian womanhood. Her presidential address was widely applauded as the Charter of National liberty. While analysing the causes of awakening of a new spirit in India, she included the awakening of women also as one of the potent factors responsible for the vigorous political stir in the country.

Referring to the Indian women's movement she said, "deep in the heart of India's daughters arose their mother's voice, calling on them to help, to arise and to be once more mistress in her own house." It was on Annie Besant's call that many women joined the Home Rule Movement and they could no more remain indifferent to the problem of India's freedom. She said, "The strength of the movement is rendered ten-fold greater by the adhesion to it of a large number of women, who bring to its help the incalculative heroism, the endurance, the self sacrifice, of the feminine nature.... Our league's best recruits and recruiters are among the women of India."

With a few other important women of the time, Annie Besant laid the foundation of Women's Indian Association. It became the pivot around which women could gather to discuss and demand their rights. Mrs. Besant went to England as a representative of the Indian women to give evidence before the Joint Parliamentary Committee, in favour of women's franchise. There she exercised her influence on British public opinion and the Parliament to see that Indian women got the franchise right along with the men.

Annie Besant was against the custom of child-marriage. She did not encourage admission of the married girls to the Hindu College, Banaras. She favoured widow re-marriage only in case of the child-widow. However she did not approve of re-marriage for adult widows. She also condemned women's seclusion and gave a clarion call to the women to arise, awake, act and attain all that the glorious female ancestors in the Rigvedic period had. She said: "The future of India depends on the abolition of child marriage amongst the people; as long as that persists, there are certain inevitable consequences of lowered vitality, of the spread of nervous diseases, of premature old age, all of which you can see going in India of to-day, standing in the way of her taking place among the physically stronger nations of the world." She added that, "It makes marriage a commercial contract or a union of bodies only, as well disintegrating the sacred life of the family which is the dearest pride of Indian women." She envisaged the foundation of a new India, built upon the joint endeavours of men and women both.

Annie Besant, as the first President of the Women's Indian Association, gave a powerful lead to the women's movement in India. She rightly was the torch-bearer and the true inspirer, who effortlessly took up the reins of the movement and led it to the desired goal. C.M. Reddi rightly observes that "Dr. Annie Besant prepared the ground for the Gandhian Freedom Movement in which the Indian women played a prominent part." She always advised the Indian women that, "For India's uplift, women must have an open field, unfettered hands, and unimpeded activity. The two sexes were not evolved for that one should enslave the other, but that they should utilize the fuller life, the differences which pertain to sex. Womanhood as well as manhood must be consecrate to the motherland, for in their union lie the strength, the stability and freedom of India."

M.E. Cousins was one of the most illustrious women

leaders who played an important role in shaping the women's movement in India. Like Mrs. Besant, she too was an Irish lady deeply interested in the progress of India and her homeland. She was born at Boyle (Ireland) in 1878. She matriculated with distinction from Londonberry Girls' High School and specialized in a course of Music from Royal Irish Academy of Music. In 1903, she married Dr. J. Cousins. She founded the Irish Women's Franchise League and devoted considerable time to the Women Suffrage Movement in England and Ireland. In 1915, she was keenly interested in the propagation of female education in India. In 1916, she was elected as the first non-Indian member of the Indian Women's University Association of Poona. In 1917, when the Women's Indian Association was founded, she was elected as Joint Secretary.

She was the Editor of *Stri Dharma,* the magazine published by the Association. M.E. Cousins travelled far and wide in the country to study the nature, temperament and problems of the Indian women. She raised her voice in unequivocal terms for reinstating the Indian women to the position of ancient glory. She was in favour of giving full opportunity of development to every woman.

The idea of 'Vote for Women' agitation first originated with her as a result of a casual conversation with her husband. An ardent suffragist, Mrs. Cousins successfully took up this task for the Indian women. She wrote,—"Within my first year of landing on Indian soil, I was dedicated to the service of India via service to that half of India—its womanhood—the problems of womanhood could be solved most fundamentally and successfully with the millennia old spiritual ideals of India."

Mrs. Cousins organized public meetings, wrote petitions, sent deputations and made appeals to the members of the respective councils and pressurized prominent men and women of every province to support the Bill. Later, she wrote, "We have worked long and strenuously in educating men through the National Congress and other political federations and the justice of women's suffrage is now almost universally admitted among men."

The great task which Margaret Cousins began, involved huge correspondence and wide travelling in the country which meant heavy expenditure. She approached many an International Association for financial help. The Leslie Commission for women's Suffrage came to her rescue and financed the movement started by her. Mrs. Cousins made it a point to be personally present in the visitor's galleries of provincial Assemblies whenever the resolutions pertaining to women's franchise were introduced.

While conducting the Women Suffrage campaign in Bihar, she boldly declared, "It has never been the tradition or custom of India to make the 'sex' a limitation or prohibition in the service of her country.... The present disqualification is a purely modern and western importation."

She was a bitter critic of the social maladies from which the Indian women suffered. She clearly pointed out that the most difficult struggle on the part of women was to be directed against women themselves. She suggested that "woman must conquer timidity, shyness, sensitiveness, shrinking from insult, real or fancied. She must conquer self-depreciation, she must learn impersonality, she must study her subject." She wrote to the Leslie Commission that "The need in India is perhaps greater than in any other country, against such evils as child marriage, education of widows, etc., and to gain many pressing reforms such as primary and higher education for girls, to reduce the terrible infant mortality and so many more things."

In 1926, Margaret Cousins founded the All India Women's Conference along with Sarojini Naidu. It became the main forum for women to plead for social reforms and the progress of female education. On a visit to USA along with her husband, she got an opportunity to attend the session of Pan Pacific Women's Conference. When she returned to India, she was able to plan an All Asian Women's Conference on the model of Pan Pacific Conference and could enlarge the scope of her work to the whole of Asia. She provided the Indian women with an opportunity to serve their sisters belonging to other parts of the Continent also. She raised large funds and laboured hard to make the Asian Conference a grand success. She wrote two valuable books—'Awakening of Asian Womanhood' and 'Indian Womanhood Today', which were highly applauded. After coming out of imprisonment in the year 1930, she made an extensive tour of the country. Her contribution to shaping the Indian feminism is indeed immeasurable and highly commendable.

Born in 1872, Sarla Devi was the daughter of Swarnakumari Devi, the elder sister of Rabindra Nath Tagore. After completing her education, she became the editor of 'Bharti' and wrote thought provoking editorials on Hindu-Muslim unity and the work of the Indian National Congress. She organized centres for physical education at Calcutta and performed religious ceremonies to honour the departed national heroes. Like her mother, she took up the cause of Swadeshi as sponsored by the Congress. She was married to Ram Bhoj Dutt Chaudhary in 1905. Her husband was a nationalist. She was a staunch follower of Arya Samaj. She founded in the year 1905 an organization known as Suhrid Samiti with a view to spiritualize the national efforts for winning freedom. She carried on extensive tours specially in Punjab, and opened Arya Samaj branches for women. Often, she gave forceful speeches in favour of female education. As the government suspected her activities to be politically motivated, she was shadowed on her tours by the officers of Criminal Investigation Department. But Sarla Devi boldly condemned them. She was very active and hard-working lady. She supervised the work of the Hindustan Press and regularly attended its office. She sponsored Essay competitions on subjects of national importance and encouraged oral discussions by holding regular meetings.

At Arya Samaj Girls School Saharanpur, she asserted that "Knowledge is the great remedy for fear. Give Knowledge to your womenfolk. Get them rid of fear and they will transmit fearlessness to your lives." She came out to be a great force in the women's movement of India. In 1910, in the face of bitter opposition, she founded "Bharat Stri Maha-Mandal". She worked as the Secretary of the organization. She inspired the women of Calcutta and Allahabad to open branches of Bharat Stri Maha-Mandal. The main object of Sarla Devi was to bring their common interest in the moral and material progress of Indian womanhood. She took an active part in the franchise movement set in motion by Mrs. Cousins. Later she conducted the movement in Bengal and succeeded in securing vote for women. She was inspired by the Non-Cooperation movement of Mahatma Gandhi and since 1919 remained an ardent Congress worker till her death in 1945.

Born in 1879, Sarojini Naidu was the daughter of Dr. Aghore Nath Chattopadhyaya, who lived in Hyderabad and established the Nizam's College. She went to England in 1895 with a state scholarship and studied for some time at the King's College, London and Girton College, Cambridge. After her return to India in 1898, she married Dr. Govindarajulu Naidu. It was an inter-caste and inter-provincial marriage.

She developed her poetic gifts and sang about the beauty of Indian landscapes, about common men and women and about the subjection of India. In her poetry, there is an exuberance of spirit. Her belief that India's future was bright even in the midst of political misfortune and disasters was unwavering.

Sarojini Naidu was happiest when she wrote her songs, but gradually she was drawn from poetry to politics. She took the lead in the women's movement. In the words of Margaret Cousins, 'Vividly an internationalist, a world citizen, the needs of India localized her activities. Supremely magnetic, with a beautiful voice, this artist made the supreme renunciation of her gift of poetry to gain the freedom of soul for Mother India. She was "The Voice of India."

Sarojini Naidu attended the Social Conference and moved a resolution for the protection of the Hindu widows in 1909. She was a great champion of female education. She believed firmly that the salvation of India was a distant dream until and unless the fallen state of women was raised by the countrymen. In 1913, she propagated the idea of Hindu-Muslim unity from the platform of All India Muslim League. She sponsored the resolution on Self-Government. She fought both for the country's freedom and for the women's right. She led the deputation of women to the Viceroy for stressing the need of socio-political progress of Indian women. In 1918, she attended the session of Indian National Congress at Bombay where she worked for getting the resolution on women's franchise passed. In 1919, she went to England as member of Home Rule League Deputation and gave evidence before the Joint Parliamentary Committee. She took the opportunity to put forward the women's case for franchise as well. She felt that without effective propaganda, the Montague Chelmsford Constitution was likely to be marked with sex-disqualifications. She, therefore, organized a powerful agitation in England and headed a joint deputation of all Indian political organizations then in England. She thus made a strong case for Women's Suffrage.

Mrs. Naidu actively participated in Mahatma Gandhi's Non-Co-operation Movement. She toured the country and delivered eloquent speeches in favour of the country's freedom laying stress on patriotism, service and dedication to the Motherland. She made special appeal to the women against the Rowlatt Act. She returned the Kaiser-i-Hind medal to the

British Government as a mark of protest. She was a great political genius and a staunch follower of Gandhiji. In 1924, she went to South Africa to study the plight of Indians in that country. In 1925 she was elected President of the Indian National Congress. She said after her election: "I am fully aware that you have bestowed upon me the richest gift. I am aware of this possession.... It is a tribute to Indian womanhood and a token of your loyal recognition of its legitimate place in the secular and spiritual councils of the Nation."

Mrs. Naidu represented the highest ideal of Indian womanhood. She visited USA and delivered about two hundred lectures there in which she interpreted Hindu womanhood and India's campaign for freedom. In 1929, when she presided over the First Provincial U.P. Youth Conference, she exhorted upon the youngmen to understand the meaning of 'give me liberty or death as the only choice left before the country.' She was specially nominated by Gandhiji to initiate the raid upon Dharasana Salt Works in May 1930. She delivered a public speech before launching the raid in which she exhorted the women to fight for the country along with men.

On the occasion of New Year, she sent a message to the Congress President, "Mine, as becomes a woman, is a most modest domestic programme merely to restore to India her true position as the supreme mistress in her own home, the sole guardian of her own vast resources and the sole dispenser of her own hospitality. As a loyal daughter of Bharat Mata, therefore, it will be my lovely though difficult task through the coming year, to set my house in order, to reconcile the tragic quarrels that threaten the integrity of her old joint family life of diverse communities and creeds and to find an adequate place and purpose and recognition alike for the lowest and highest of her children and foster children, the guests and strangers within her gate." She further said that, "The time has come in my opinion, when women can no longer seek immunity behind the shelter of their sex, but must share equally with their men comrades all the perils and sacrifices for the liberation of the country." When Gandhiji was arrested, he ordered his followers to stick to the method of peace and non-violence. Sarojini was arrested on 21st May 1930. She was released under the Gandhi-Irwin Pact. She attended the second Round Table Conference in London as an official representative of the women of India. In 1932, she became the Acting President of the Indian National Congress. She was arrested when she defied the government orders for not holding any meeting.

Mrs. Naidu worked hard to bring the Hindus and Muslims together. She was arrested after the resolution of the Quit India was passed on August 8, 1942. In spite of her shattered health, she continued her political struggle. After the country became free, she was given the privilege of being the first woman Governor of a State (Uttar Pradesh). A great champion of women's rights, she passed away in 1949. She had asserted that, "There was no power in the world that could set any limitation to women's achievements." She further said that, "One thing is unchangeable throughout the world, the indivisibility of womanhood. The frontiers, wars, races, many things make for division, but womanhood combines,—the queen and the peasant women are one, and the time has come when every woman should know her own divinity."

A number of other women workers conscientiously devoted themselves to the cause of female emancipation and feminism. Their contribution in the various fields of women's movement had been indeed immeasurable.

Mrs. Rustomji Faridoonji

She was a co-worker of M.E. Cousins and worked for the attainment of civic and political rights for women and the promotion of the right type of education for women. She served first as Vice-President and then as President of the All India Women's Conference. She was an active Secretary of the All India Education Fund Association from its very inception. She founded the famous Lady Irwin College. She was elected President of the All India Education Fund Association, the office she held till the end. M.E. Cousins observed that, "Faridoonji was one of the most impressive personalities amongst the leaders of Women's Movement. Impressive ... tall, handsome, dignified, graceful, decorative, blessed with a strong control of voice. She was a known Parsi figure in society."

Herabai Tata

Herabai Tata was the Honorary Secretary of Bombay Women's Indian Association. The Bombay branch was very influential and active. Herabai Tata was an active co-worker with Mrs. Margaret Cousins and Dr. Annie Besant in the fight for women's franchise. She organized big meetings in Bombay in order to popularize the Women's Suffrage movement. She went to England to give evidence before the Southborough Committee. She published the booklet 'Indian Women's Franchise', justifying the women's cause. Referring to the suffrage movement in Bombay she wrote that, "The representatives of the Hindu, Muslim, Christian and Zoroastrian faiths in this country once united by a common bond of love and understanding would, indeed, become mightier than an army with all its brilliant banners." Herabai Tata also organized lectures on different topics of women's welfare schemes.

S. Muthulakshmi Reddy

She was the first woman medical graduate of the Madras University. She won five gold medals and Honours for distinction in Medicine, Surgery and Midwifery. She was a distinguished medical practitioner, but she gave up her lucrative practice for social service. She began to devote her thought, time and energy for the emancipation of women and for the care and protection of children. She was associated with Women's Indian Association ever since its inception in 1917. She later became its President. She guided the policy and programme of All India Women's Conference. She was a pioneer legislator in Madras Legislature.

She was elected Deputy President of the Madras Legislative Council. In 1930, she resigned from the Council and the office of Deputy President as a protest against the arrest of Mahatma Gandhi. Dr. Reddy was requested by Mrs. Cousins to preside over the All Asian Women's Conference in 1931. She very efficiently handled the charge of President. She attended the International Conference on Women in Paris and America as a delegate from India. In 1933 she, along with Sarojini Naidu, went to tender evidence before the Joint Parliamentary Committees. In 1937, she was elected as the first Elderwoman in the City Corporation of Madras. She retained the post till 1940.

She issued a statement before her departure to London that, "I have accepted the invitation in response to the wishes of my sisters to represent the organized women's point of view before the British Public, that thinking women of India are opposed to communalism of every shape or kind, that women do not seek any safeguard or protection for themselves in the new Constitution and that the new Constitution should be based upon the sound principle of perfect sex equality and that women cannot be freed from the shackles of customs and conventions unless the men themselves are free and responsible citizens."

When Mahatma Gandhi visited Madras, she presided over the Congress Constructive Worker's Conference. In 1946, she laid the foundation of 'Awai Home' in order to help orphans and destitute women. She also established the Cancer Institute, Madras. For her meritorious services, the President of India honoured her with the award 'Padma Bhushan', in 1956.

Durgabai Deshmukh

Durgabai Deshmukh represents the Indian women's struggle for social, legal and political rights. She was born in 1909 and was married at the age of eight into a conservative family. She became a widow at an early age. She was a great patriot and even as a girl she was inspired to serve the country. At the tender age of thirteen only, she started Balika Hindi Pathshala in Kakinada. She was elected as a member of the District Board at the age of nineteen. She was full of noble impulse and zeal for service. In 1930, she participated in the Salt Satyagraha and was appointed the first woman dictator of the Salt raid in Madras.

When in jail, she learnt the English language. She led the Seva Dal at Bombay. She was again imprisoned in 1932 and sentenced to six months rigorous imprisonment. Later, she passed matriculation, BA, BL and MA examinations. She won gold medals and prizes in the University. She enrolled herself to study law. She founded a Girls' Club while studying at Law College. In her later life she laid the foundation of Andhra Mahila Sabha, Industrial Home for Women and Nurses' Training Centre at Madras.

She contested elections and was elected a member of the Central Assembly. She also served on the Constituent Assembly and actively associated herself with the work of Constitution making. She was a member of Goodwill Mission and also served as Chairman of Central Social Welfare Board.

She inspired women all over India with great enthusiasm, dauntless courage and firm conviction. She fully proved Dr. Annie Besant's conviction that the redemption and regeneration of Indians depend upon the efforts made by Indians themselves. She laid out schemes for the welfare of women and children. She acted as a member of the Planning Commission. She touched every aspect of the problems that concerned the welfare of women and children and tried her level best to draw the attention of the Government to these issues.

Raj Kumari Amrit Kaur

Raj Kumari Amrit Kaur was a princess of the Kapurthala ruling family. Educated in England, she became an eminent social worker of Punjab. In 1929, she joined the All India Women's Conference as its Secretary. Later she became its President. It was due to her practical statesmanship and wise counsel that the All India Women's Conference safely steered through the difficult period of political unrest. Her intelligence and convincing evidence in support of Women's Memorandum for equal rights and status in the new Constitution deeply impressed the Lothian Committee about the capabilities of Indian women. She also went to London to give evidence before the Joint Parliamentary Committee in 1932.

She became a loyal disciple of Mahatma Gandhi and worked as his trusted Secretary for a number of years. She was imprisoned in 1942 for her political activities.

After independence, she was elected to the Lok Sabha from Punjab Constituency by majority votes. She became the first woman Health Minister of the Indian Union. She initiated schemes for the expansion of Maternity and Child Welfare, training of nurses, control of malaria, filaria, venereal diseases, leprosy, tuberculosis, cancer, etc., and took measures for improving national health. It was at her initiative that the All India Medical Institute was established at Delhi for training and research of scholars and for promoting post-graduate medical education. She was responsible for the allocation of funds in the Second Five Year

Plan for research in leprosy, T.B. and cancer. Raj Kumari Amrit Kaur's distinguished service in the World Health Organization and allied UN International Assemblies and Associations brought financial help to Indian people. The medical and other scientific equipments to the Indian Hospitals could be obtained only because of her unique efforts. She was a great woman leader.

Vijay Lakshmi Pandit

Daughter of Pandit Moti Lal Nehru, V.L. Pandit was born in 1900. She first attended the Congress Session in 1919 at Amritsar presided over by her father. She was married in 1921. She took an active part in the Civil Disobedience Movement of 1930 and 1931-32. She was arrested in 1932. In 1935, she fought elections of the Allahabad Municipal Committee. She was elected Chairman of the Education Committee.

She contested elections in 1936 from Kanpur. She was appointed Health Minister when the Congress formed the ministry in Uttar Pradesh in 1936. As minister, she did memorable work in the field of Health and Education. She actively participated in the 'Quit India Movement' of 1942 and was imprisoned. After her release, she went to America and upheld the cause of India's freedom. She was highly admired by the Americans. She presented a comprehensive Memorandum for the liberty of India at San Francisco Conference. She spoke not only for India but also for the six hundred million people of India and South East Asia.

She won unopposed to the Uttar Pradesh Legislative Assembly and became a minister for Local Self-Government and Health Department during 1946-47. She led India's delegation to the United Nations Assembly in 1946, 1947 and 1948. From the year 1940 to 1942 Mrs. Pandit was the President of All India Women's Conference. She was the first woman to be elected as President of the United Nations

Assembly in 1953—a unique honour for Indian womanhood indeed! She served as India's High Commissioner in London and also worked as Ambassador to Russia.

She emerged as a great feminist and a real genius. She proved to the world that women also could be as successful world statesmen and diplomats as men.

Kamla Devi Chattopadhyaya

She was born in Mangalore in 1903 and was married at an early age. She became a child widow. She continued her studies and joined Queen Mary's College at Madras. She later married Harindra Nath Chattopadhyaya and presented a model of inter-caste, inter-provincial widow-marriage. She was the first woman to contest elections to the Legislative Assembly in 1926.

Kamla Devi was associated with many women's organizations. In 1929, she attended the International Congress of Women's League for Peace and Freedom in Prague. She actively participated in the Civil Disobedience Movement. She addressed meetings, and picketed shops of foreign cloth and liquor. She prepared and sold salt even in the High Court premises. She toured the whole of India and established *Seva Dal* in different parts of the country. She was incharge of the women's wing of this organization. She prescribed training for the literary education of girls along with domestic hygiene, child rearing, sewing and spinning. She taught them to organize meetings and inspired them to study history and geography so that they became fit for all that the country expected of them. Kamla Devi was the Chairman of Bombay Youth League. She was imprisoned in 1932. After her release, she joined the Congress Socialist Party.

Her work in the field of women's movement was quite successful. She wrote a number of articles on the status and position of women.

Begum Sharifa Hamid Ali

Begum Sharifa Hamid Ali was the champion of Hindu-Muslim unity and an eminent social worker. She was a nationalist Muslim. She was the President of the All India Women's Conference for many years. She also gave evidence before the Joint Parliamentary Committee of the Round Table Conference in London in 1932-33, on the Memorandum of the All India Women's Conference for joint electorates, adult suffrage and Committee of the UNO on Human Rights.

Lady Sadasiva Iyer

Lady Managlanmal Sadasiva Iyer was the wife of Sir T. Sadasiva Iyer, an eminent judge of the Madras High Court. She had to live in orthodox surroundings and faced adverse criticism of family members for her participation in public life. She was a delegate to the first All India Women's Conference held at Poona in 1927. She later became an active member of the Association. She earned prestige and popularity as a practical reformer, a fluent and impressive speaker in almost all the regional languages of the South. She was one of the members of the women's deputation that waited upon Sir Montague, and she later became the Vice-president of the Women's Indian Association. She stood for the complete emancipation of Indian women in all spheres of activities.

Cornelia Sorabjee

Cornelia Sorabjee was a very intelligent lady. She distinguished herself in School and College as a brilliant scholar. In 1887, she topped the merit list of the University. She served the Gujarat College for men at Ahmedabad as an efficient professor of English. She sailed for England to obtain higher degree in Law. On her return, she visited

Bengal at the invitation of the Indian Female School and Zenana Missionary Society. She was appointed as Legal Adviser for women in *Purdah* by the Government of Bengal. She believed that only through development and progress of education, the country's betterment would follow. She wrote an article, "Stray Thoughts of an Indian Girl in the Nineteenth Century." She arrived at the conclusion that everything might best be left to education. She also warned the reformers for their over zealous advocacy and over-doing of the traditional life in India.

Almost in all parts of the country, enlightened and intelligent women came forward to share, in the broader perspective, the fruits of the feminist movement. They were—Mrs. C. Jinarajadasa, Rani Lakshmi Bai Rajwade, Dr. (Miss) Joshi, Mrs. Sarla Bai Naik, Mrs. Srirangamma, Mrs. Lazarus, Mrs. Chandra Shekhar Aiyar, Mrs. Dalvi, Begum Hasrat Mohani, Mrs. Guruswami Chetty, Miss H. Petite, Mrs. Nilkanta, Mrs. Uma Nehru, Miss Arundale, Mrs. Padma Bai Sanjiva Rao, Miss Gokhale, Lady Dhunbai Cowasji Jehangir, Mrs. A. Swaminathan, Mrs. Rukmani Lakshmipalli, Maharani Chimnabai Gaekwad of Baroda, Lady Jagdish Chandra Bose, Mrs. Radhabai Subharoyan, Begum Shah Nawaz, Maharani Setu Parvati Bayi of Travancore, the Princess Durre Shewar, Mrs. Brijlal Nehru, Smt. Bharati Ranga, Aruna Asaf Ali, Jayashri Raiji, Mrs. Kamalamma Dasappa, Begum Sultan Mir Amiruddin, Begum Attiya Habibullah, Maniben Kara, Mrs. Leila Mani Naidu, Mrs. Billimora, Miss Gupta of Lahore, Miss Mridula Sarabhai, Miss Bharati Sarabhai, Mrs. Lakshmi Menon, Begum Mirza Ismail and Mrs. Karimbhai. All these women were responsible for the fast growth of feminism in the country. All the enlightened women were united together and they walked together on the road to plenty, peace and prosperity.

The selfless services rendered by the women leaders to the cause of Indian womanhood is not only praise-worthy, but it has also an intrinsic value in itself. They laid stress on the grave social problems of the day and did yeoman task by impressing upon the Government, the need for social progress of women. They contributed to various journals and compiled books on the socio-economic problems. They attracted the attention of not only the Indians but also of the people of different countries who were sympathetic to the cause of Indian womanhood. Many of the women leaders adopted a policy of vigorous propaganda and they could easily maintain a link with various international organizations of women. They conducted their activities through different women's organizations, and became responsible for various social legislations passed by the government with reference to women. Almost all of them favoured the growth and development of female education in the country. A few of them founded schools and colleges with an improved syllabus and teaching programme, that suited the respectable vocations and temperament of the Indian women.

These outstanding personalities led to a commotion in the different spheres of public activity. They took up the cause of the country, along with the cause of women. They gallantly suffered privations, tortures and imprisonment at the hands of the British government. Their active participation in the National Movement belied the old theory of their perpetual tutelage. There emerged a free, strong and courageous image of Indian womanhood. All these women showed extra-ordinary capacities and capabilities in all walks of life. As such they came to be widely acknowledged as the 'useful' members of society. They became alive not only to the national but also to the international problems of their time.

It is true that all their efforts were practically confined to the women of higher and the middle classes and could not reach to the women masses of India. As they themselves belonged to urban areas, they could hardly understand the concerns of rural women of the country who also needed their attention and advice.

Besides, they laid emphasis on the female education and did not bother about other problems concerning women's life. Probably they thought that education was the only remedy to all the existing maladies of women. With the rapid progress of female education in the urban areas and no provision for the women in the villages, there came to exist a wide chasm between the western-minded educated and enlightened Indian women and the uneducated, innocent and traditional women of the rural regions. This gulf exists even today. They were so much absorbed in enjoying the outcome of western education that the problems of rural and uneducated women masses were completely lost sight of. They failed to identify the Indian womanhood and its real problems as a compact unit. This drawback remained from the very beginning of Indian feminism. The movement remained a class movement which ought to have been a mass movement taking in its fold the all embracing programme of upliftment of general women even of the rural areas.

Another fact that strikes most is the harm caused to women's movement by their involvement in the political movement and the national struggle. The energy and time of the women leaders were diverted towards the fight for freedom. As a result, they could not attain much for their own movement. Yet it was their quality and calibre in patriotism that they felt more for their country than anything else.

It is true that the feminist movement in the country yielded remarkable results and the women who worked for it unanimously agreed never to differ on petty questions of caste, colour or creed. Though some favourable rights were acquired by the women of India even under the patriarchal system, yet there existed a big gap between theory and practice. They continued their struggle for acquiring the actual rights that could be effective and real.

6. Towards Fulfilment

Many of the educated and enlightened women established local and national organizations to speed up the feminist movement. They began to carry out solid and constructive programmes of their own kind. The women leaders were determined to bring about the programme of socio-political and cultural advancement. This development, indeed, marked a mature stage in the evolution of feminism in India. These socio-religious organizations played some role in promoting female education and in the eradication of social evils like purdah, child-marriage and polygamy. They also advocated widow-marriage and worked constantly to improve the degraded condition of women. The promise of a bright and brilliant future awaited the Indian womanhood as the women leaders themselves came forward to establish these organizations to provide them with the opportunity to seek and evolve the true path of their own redemption. The educated women realized their responsibility and considered it their duty to give proper guidance and training to the general womenfolk to broaden their outlook. The members of these organizations were inspired by the high ideals of ancient Indian culture. These organizations included those which were established before the first World War when scattered attempts were made by individual women leaders to change the social status of Indian women. Other organizations were founded after 1918 when as a result of a wide awakening among women themselves, they carried out a definite programme of social work and education. They were infused with a spirit of neo-awakening. These organizations worked for the general progress and their total metamorphosis. All these organizations were run by women themselves.

In 1886, Swarna Kumari Debi founded, under the auspices of Brahmo Samaj, a Ladies' Association with the object of promoting friendly relations among Indian ladies and fostering in them the spirit of service for the political welfare of the country. The Association also made provisions for a Rescue Home for imparting shelter and education to the poor girls. The Zenana teachers were sent after proper training and education to educate the house-wives.

In 1884, Swarna Kumari Devi herself discarded Purdah and edited *Bamabodhini Patrika*. She became the President of the Ladies section of the Theosophical Society of Bengal in 1885-86. She attended the session of Indian National Congress in 1900 as a delegate from Bengal. Referring to her services, Amiya Bhusan Basu said, "Her early efforts in improving the condition of womenfolk in Bengal, when the outlook was gloomy and opposition was so strong, remind us of what Emerson had said once that 'there is always room for a man of force and he makes room for many'."

Pandita Ramabai founded Sharda Sadan in 1892 as the nucleus for higher education for girls. It was a remarkable organization to serve the needy and destitute women. Padmini Sen Gupta remarks, "Like buds opening their petals, the girls began to expand, learning to appreciate the cult of service and unselfish sacrifice which Ramabai inculcated." Ramabai later expanded the field of social service. She included famine relief programme by the Sadan and opened an institution for the orphans. Her greatest achievement was the establishment of Mukti Sadan in 1898 for the welfare of helpless women and children.

In the memory of an ardent social reformer Mahipatram, an organization was started at Ahmedabad in 1892 with the aim of giving shelter to illegitimate and deserted children and the pregnant women moving in a helpless state.

It also admitted widows and other destitute women who were not capable of maintaining themselves. They were trained in the various crafts and were taught to be self-supporting. It also helped the widows in their efforts to stand on their own feet. The Ashram was working in different areas of activity very efficiently.

In 1903, the Parsi women of Bombay founded Stree Zoroastrian Mandal. They formulated a scheme of first visiting poor women and emphasizing upon them the value of constructive work in life. They inspired poor women to work in different cottage industries so that they might stop living on doles or charity and may get not only economic relief but economic independence. They also distributed medicines, food and milk among poor Parsi families. The organization performed good work in the field of education and self-help programmes.

An eminent social worker of Bombay, B.N. Motiwala, founded the Gujarati Hindu Stri Mandal in 1908. His idea was to give training to the Gujarati women in domestic arts as well as in education. The objectives of the Mandal were to encourage contact among the women and to provide them with appropriate education and vocation. The organization stood for the elevation of the status of women with regard to their domestic, economic, moral and political spheres. It organized classes for sewing, embroidery, painting, leather work and provided regular teaching to them. It held classes in Gujarati language, English literature, Sanskrit, Hindi and Music. The Mandal later started a Girls' Association and formed different committees for cultural attainments. It also started a library and published a monthly bulletin to report its activities to the public.

Established by Ramabai Ranade in 1909, the Seva Sadan provided a home for women with facility of education. It prepared them even for social work. The Sadan started classes in industrial training for adult women, a Teacher's training College, and a High School. It opened a medical department and nurses centre. Referring to the contribution of Mrs. Ranade in the field of women's organization, M.S. Vidwan says, "Her achievements symbolize a glorious transition in the women's movement." He writes that "From the cloistered virtues of the past, they marched towards an ideal in which women would be an equal partner with men in all spheres of activity.... Due to her efforts the Seva Sadan became an active movement."

A devoted social worker and a representative of Indian womanhood, Saroj Nalini woke up her sisters from deep slumber and called upon them to organize Mahila Samitis in every district, town and villages in order to educate the women. Many associations sprang up in Bengal as a result of her sincere efforts. These organizations took steps to abolish purdah and infant marriages, and encouraged widow re-marriage. The members of these Samitis worked hard to enlighten the women on health and sanitation, and pleaded for equal socio-political rights in education and franchise.

In Poona, with the aim to serve the society in general and women and children in particular, the Bhagini Samaj was established in 1916. The aim of this organization was to elevate the status of Indian women in the new socio-economic set-up of the country. Its programme included education, social service, propaganda and legal work. It organized classes for adult women, night classes for working women and made medical facilities available to the poorer classes of the society. Later, it started co-operative stores and organized exhibitions of their products.

In 1914, the Chimnabai Maternity and Child Welfare League was started to look after the health of the women of poor localities. In 1940, Saroj Nalini wrote about these organizations in the book "Women of India," published from London, as under:

> "Thy dear Samithis loving call
> Has roused the slumbering women of the land
> From a hundred thousand homes they gather forth
> Their mission to fulfil for the nation's good."

Another organization, "Udyogalaya" was organized to train the middle class and working class women in some crafts in order to make them self-reliant. It organized classes in sewing, embroidery, book-binding, calico-printing, carpet-making, weaving and cooking. The Baroda Stree Sahakari Stores Ltd. was established for the sale of the finished goods on co-operative basis. It tried to foster amongst the members, a sense of economy and encouraged the use of Swadeshi in their life.

In May 1917, the Women Indian Association was founded. It was the first organization which aimed to have an all-India scope. It included among its members all women, who were intellectually aware and bound them together in mutual service and the welfare of the country. It was the first organization which aimed at creating an overall awakening among women, while training them to shoulder their responsibilities in public service. It had a non-sectarian character and it included in its fold the women belonging to all classes and enrolled them without any distinction of caste, colour or religion. Its branches were first opened at Srinagar, Madras, Calicut, Tanjore, Bezwada and Bombay. Later, its branches were extended to other parts of India. Its first President was Mrs. Annie Besant, and for eight years, Mrs. Dorothy Jinarjadasa remained its honorary Secretary. The Association, under the inspiring leadership of M.E. Cousins, conducted the Women's Suffrage Movement and succeeded in its mission. The Women Indian Association appealed to the enlightened members of the Council for help in the task of the Women's Suffrage Movement and maintained regular contact with various international organizations for financial assistance. The inclusion of women candidates in the Council became its main motive. It also asserted for equal political rights of women. Mrs. Cousins wrote to an important member of Madras Council that, "the electoral rolls have been amended for Legislative bodies regarding the removal of the sex disqualification. We feel that it is a matter of urgency that the resolution should include in the Legislative Council, able women to be either nominated or elected as its members."

Many women organizations were established after the end of the Great War. These organizations were based on broad principles and liberal objectives of general welfare and an all round development not only of the womenfolk but of the entire country.

Women's Council of India and All India Women's Conference

Founded in 1920 at Bombay, the membership of Women's Council of India was open to all women engaged or linked with women's work. It also extended its affiliation to other women's organizations. This Council was designed to act as a co-ordinating and directing body for all social and philanthropic work conducted for the welfare of women and children throughout the Bombay Presidency. It was meant to be "a rallying ground for all organized efforts." It conducted the functions of the Home Industries Children's Holiday Library, Labour Camps, and Parliamentary Sub-committee. It dealt with the beggar problem and the Literacy movement. In 1922, the Council opened the Rescue Home for women. The object was to provide relief to the fallen women and girls and to offer shelter to stranded women.

Feminism in India passed through various stages of development. Started by the worthy women leaders, it reached its fulfilment in 1926, when the All India Women's Conference was established. It became the most outstanding all India organization of the Indian women to fight for their rights and work for their general welfare and promotion of female education. The stimulus for the establishment of the Conference came from an appeal made by Mr. Oaten, the Director of Public Instructions in Bengal, at a function of the Bethune College, Calcutta. As the chief guest, he called upon the Indian women "to tell with one voice what they want and keep on telling us till they got it." Lady Huidekoper published two articles in "Stree Dharma" on the inspiring address of the Director. On the basis of these articles, M. Cousins circulated a letter in which she appealed to the educated women of India to lay the foundation of an all India organization for themselves.

Addressing the women, she said, "you have asserted yourselves in the field of politics. How long you shall take to assert yourselves in the field of secondary and higher education? How long are you going to tolerate a man-made syllabus, a man-made system, a man-made examination, and a controlling authority in which women have no influence as the dominating arbiter of your educational destinies?... We must have the co-operation of women to help us, and to seek the remedy." She further suggested to the Indian women that, "I would urge that women, who alone can help us adequately, should tell us with one voice what they want, and keep on telling us till they get it. "She advised the educated women of the country to form local committees to be subsequently synthesized into an All India Organization. They were called upon to express their views on female education and help to formulate a concrete scheme. Her appeal was met with a wide and enthusiastic response and a series of Conferences were held at twenty two different places in India between the months of September and December of the year 1926. The deliberations led to the foundation of All India Women's Conference. The first session of AIWC was held at Poona from January 5th to January 8th, 1927 under the Presidentship of Her Highness, the Maharani Chimnabai Gaekwad of Baroda.

Mrs. Cousins later observed that "The Conference has been a historic event. It has marked the opening of a new era in the evolution of education in India by its insistence on the inclusion of moral training, based on spiritual ideals, in all schools and colleges, and by all students." It particularly suggested to make the primary education compulsory for all the girls.

In 1927, Mr. Margaret Cousins was elected the first Honorary Organizing Secretary of AIWC. The resolutions passed at the first Conference related, almost without any exception, to the question of women's education from primary to higher education. A notable exception was the resolution condemning the practice of early marriage, as it interfered with education. They supported the Hari Singh Gour's Age of Consent Bill which was then about to come before the Legislative Assembly. The first Conference concentrated upon laying the foundation stone of the educational edifice for the women.

M.E. Cousins later wrote:

> "The Conference has thus been the result of constant work since the 28th June, 1926 in response to the appeal to women of the Bengal Director of Public Instruction, to express women's views on education. The appeal was reiterated by A.L. Huidekoper through the women's magazine "Stri Dharma" broadcast and answered by the enthusiastic local women leaders in the twentytwo Constituent Conferences and finally by the All India Constituent bodies of the Delegates of which this Report

gives but an adequate resume."

The Conference inspired the women young and old, into a bond of spiritual sisterhood, dedicated and sent forth to turn their vision into accomplishment and to embody the general principles suggested by them into a detailed system of a new Educational-Social Era for Indian feminism.

The second Conference was held at Delhi in 1928 under the presidentship of the Begum mother of Bhopal. The proceedings were opened by Lady Irwin. The most interesting resolution passed during this Conference related to Rai Har Bilas Sarda's Bill for the restraint of the custom of early marriage. Another notable resolution urged the government to give representation to women in the Central Legislature. During this Conference an All India Women's Education Fund was created from which Lady Irwin College was later founded. The third Conference was held at Patna in 1929, with the Dowager Rani of Mandi as the President. For the first time the Conference included social reforms in its deliberations and a separate section was created to deal with social problems of the day.

The Fourth Conference was held at Bombay in 1930 and was presided over by Mrs. Sarojini Naidu. Prominent among the list of reforms introduced through the support of the Conference was the passing of the Sarda Act. The success inspired the members to take an active part in the agitation for reform of the Laws of Inheritance as it affected the women. A new field of activity was included in its fold when deliberations were held on the problem of women labour. Some distinguished members appeared before the Labour Commission to give evidence. They also represented the case of Indian women in the International Conferences, such as, the Equal Citizenship Conference. The Conference appointed an all India Committee to investigate the suitable educational curriculum for girls. It conducted its meeting at Panchmarhi,

M.P., in July 1930 and drafted its final report successfully.

In 1931 with Dr. (Mrs.) Muthulakshmi Reddy in the chair, the annual Conference was held at Lahore. The enthusiasm of the members reached its peak when they observed 1st March 1931 as the 'Women's Day'. Almost all the branches of All India Women's Conference held meetings on that day. They explained the objective of the Conference in detail and popularized its programme among the public. The members carried on vigorous propaganda against the designs of orthodox sections of the Hindu community to amend the Sarda Act. The members of the Baroda branch influenced the State officials to take the lead in putting on the Statute book, 'a Divorce Act' for the Hindu women. Some branches, specially one at Madras, took up the work of abolishing untouchability and caste prejudices.

The Sixth Session of the All India Women's Conference was held in 1932 at Madras. It was presided over by Mrs. P.K. Ray. Though earlier, the Conference by its Constitution was not entitled to deal with the political issues, it ultimately became evident in the successive deliberations, that women could not be installed in their rightful position unless India becomes a free and independent country.

With the changing scene on the political horizon of the country, it was felt that status of women in the new Constitution, particularly in relation to their fundamental rights, their representation in various bodies and the conditions of their franchise-were matters of vital importance for the whole of the country. The members of the Conference felt that every opportunity must be taken to enforce their views before the new Constitution was actually drawn up in detail. For this, in April 1931, a representative meeting was held in Bombay with Mrs. Sarojini Naidu in the Chair. The All India Women's Conference, the Women's Indian Association, and the National Council of Women's India jointly drew up a Memorandum to be placed before the Franchise Sub-

Committee of the Round Table Conference. Other branches approved this step, introducing the new policy of political participation of women. The characteristic features of their demands were as follows:

1. Equal rights and obligation for all citizens without any bar on account of sex;
2. No disability to be attached to any citizen by reasons of his or her religion, caste, creed or sex in regard to public employment, office of power or honour, and for joining any trade or calling;
3. The demand of Adult Suffrage as a general rule;
4. The women should be entitled to fight elections on equal terms with men, in mixed general electorates;
5. No reservation of seats for women as such, nor special nomination or co-option.

A deputation of All India Women's Conference called on His Excellency, The Viceroy, in 1932, and presented a Memorandum demanding that women must be represented at the Round Table Conference. They also supported Rai Saheb Harbilas Sarda's Bill to secure a share for Hindu widows in their husband's family property. The Education Committee worked with unabated vigour for Home Science Education to be provided to girls in every school.

In 1933, the Seventh Conference met at Lucknow. It was presided over by Lady Vidaygauri Ramanbhay Nilkanth. The Standing Committee under the Chair-womanship of Rajkumari Amrit Kaur felt it obligatory to press for the political views as presented in the Memorandum to the Round Table Conference. In this context, M.E. Cousins wrote that "this was the most representative Association of Indian women by that time. It voiced women's demands to be included in the new form of the Indian Constitution that there should be no communal electorates, there should be only general electorates and there should be no reserved seats for women. There should be no nominated seats, that mere wifehood of a man voter should not be a qualification for a woman voter."

The Conference deliberated upon the establishment of Lady Irwin College and asserted that its aim was to enable women to utilize the advantages of Science in their homes and to add on to the loveliness of handicrafts interwoven with that particular heritage which has been embodied in India's own culture and tradition, in its national games, dances and aspirations. In November 1932, the Lady Irwin College was founded with the faculty of Home Science. The Communal Award was opposed by all sections of AIWC. Some of the members of All India Women's Conference contested elections with men on equal terms for academic posts of the Universities.

The Eighth session was held at Calcutta in 1933. Lady Abdul Qadir presided over the Conference. The publication of a White Paper revealed that all attempts made in 1931 and 1932 to gain equal status for women were falsified. This necessitated the submission of a second Memorandum before the Joint Parliamentary Committee of the British Parliament. Consequently three elected representatives of the AIWC and the Women's Indian Association were invited to London to give evidence before the Committee. Taking a firm stand, the delegation stressed that though the Indian women were ready to adopt an accommodating attitude during the period of transition, yet they firmly stood by the principle of equal status, and they resented any kind of communal or special representation. The special feature of the year 1932 was the contacts of the AIWC delegates unit with women's organizations of other countries and with such international organizations as were connected with the League of Nations that included women's welfare in their programmes.

Under the presidentship of Rustamji Faridoonji, at Karachi, the Ninth session of the All India Women's

Conference was organized successfully. The special visitors to this session were Dr. Mande Royden and Mrs. Corbett Ashby. The Conference raised over thirty thousand rupees for Bihar Earthquake Relief Fund. It was decided that efforts should be made to impress upon the British Parliament, the unanimous opinion of Indian women that neither the communal electorate, nor any wifehood qualifications should be imposed upon them. A copy of the resolution was presented to the Secretary of State for India and this resolution was reiterated unanimously at the half-yearly meeting of AIWC.

The Conference made a successful attempt to create a widespread demand for the appointment of a Commission on the legal disabilities of Indian women that would suggest reforms in the light of the current condition. An All India Day was organized on November 24, 1934 and meetings were held in every Constituent branches. Thousands of signatures were collected by the members to support their demand. A Committee was appointed to investigate the condition of women labourers, specially those who worked in mines. Besides, the Conference also appointed Rajkumari Amrit Kaur as the Liaison Officer to maintain contact with the British Women's Organizations on a permanent basis and with other international organizations of women in Europe and USA.

In December 1935, the Tenth session of AIWC was held in Trivandrum. Maharani Setu Parvati Bai of Travancore presided over the Conference. Many distinguished women from USA, China, Japan and England came to attend this session. The notable feature of this session was the work done by the Sub-committee on the Child-Marriage Restraint Act. It issued a bulletin giving statistics of child-marriage in the country. The Conference suggested many changes in the Sarda Act. Mr. B. Das was allowed to introduce the Bill for amendments in Legislative Assembly which gave due emphasis on the changes suggested by the Conference. The Conference collected funds for Earthquake Relief and displayed its awakened attitude towards the problems of natural calamities. The Liaison unit of the Conference worked hard to elicit public opinion in England. Another important work was the resolution passed to agree with the powers granted to them by the Act. The Conference also showed interest for Birth Control measures through recognized clinics and medical aid for Indian women.

The Eleventh session was held at Ahmedabad in 1936. Mrs. M.E. Cousins, its founder, was in the Chair. The progress of the Conference was visible when overseas visitors from England, Australia, USA and Holland attended the session in large numbers. The AIWC was recognized as the truly representative body and a fully established women's organization in India and abroad. The Conference had carried out extensive propaganda from press and various platforms in support of the Social Bills. The Conference enlisted public support for Dr. Deshmukh's Bill to amend the Hindu Law governing Hindu Women's rights to Property and Mr. B. Das's Bill to amend the Sarda Act in order to make it more stringent. Bhagwan Das's Bill seeking recognition of intercaste marriage and Mr. Hafiz Abdullah's Muslim's Personal Law Application Bill were whole-heartedly supported. At the request of the International Alliance of Women for Suffrage and Equal Citizenship and Educational Status of Women in India, the drafts were submitted to the League of Nations and the Government of India both.

The Twelfth session of the All India Women's Conference was held at Nagpur in December 1936. Raj Kumari Amrit Kaur was in the chair. She placed on record the glorious achievement of 60 women entering the Legislatures of the various provinces. One among them, Smt. Vijaylakshmi Pandit was raised to the status of a Cabinet Minister. It was indeed a sound proof of the strides made by the Women's movement in the country. A few of them were elected as Deputy Speakers of the different Legislatures and some of them were appointed Parliamentary Secretaries. The Standing Committee of the Conference drafted a scheme for introducing legislations to improve the social status of women and forwarded it to the Chief Ministers of the new Provincial Governments and to the women members of the Legislatures. The Conference expressed deep concern over the legal disabilities of women. Mrs. S.C. Mukherji, who was an ex-Chairman of the Standing Committee, was sent by the Government of India as Indian delegate to the Conference of the Central Authorities of the League of Nations in Eastern Countries for Combating Traffic in Women and Children held at Bandung, Java, in February 1937. It was indeed the acknowledgement of womens' capabilities.

In 1938, the thirteenth session of the Conference was held at Delhi. Rani Lakshmibai Rajwade was in the Chair. Many distinguished visitors from different countries attended the session and praised the all-round progress made by the All India Women's Conference towards a successful feminist movement in India. For the first time it was decided to publish a Journal of All India Women's Conference. The All India Women's Conference continued its constructive work. It published the four issues of the Bulletins including a supplement on Education and Health. The Fifteenth session was held at Bangalore in 1940 under the Presidentship of Smt. Rameshwari Nehru. Many delegates from Ceylon attended the Conference and gave useful suggestions.

Miss Mary A. Dingman, President of the Peace and Disarmament Committee of the International Women's Organization, Mile P. Hage of the International Labour Office, Mrs. G.F. Grag of Australia and Miss Agathe Harrison of England attended the Conference.

The Report of this session was revealing in respect of the progress that the various branches had made in different programmes of the Conference. The Government was forced to appoint a Committee to examine the injustice done to Hindu women under the old Law. The Conference strongly protested against the limitations imposed on the terms of reference for the Committee so appointed. The Journal of the Conference *Roshni* continued to render valuable services to members under the editorship of Smt. Lakshmi N. Menon.

The Sixteenth Conference of AIWC met in 1941. It was presided over by Smt. Vijaylakshmi Pandit. The scope of the Conference was enlarged when it included Village Reconstruction Project and the scheme of starting a Training camp for Provincial Organisers and other women workers in its purview. The record of the work for the year 1941 showed that all branches worked hard for the spread of literacy among women, specially adult literacy. The branches sensitively reacted to the consolidated Programmes of AIWC drawn by its Central Office at Delhi.

The Seventeenth session of the Conference met in Bombay in April 1944. It was presided over by Smt. Kamladevi Chattopadhyaya and 205 delegates attended the session. According to the amended Constitution of the Conference, all branches were placed on equal status. The annual report recorded the programme for Training of Women for Social Service. Fortynine women received training for three months. The Conference conducted an agitation in support of the Hindu Law Committee. It also undertook relief work during the floods and famines in different parts of the country. The Conference conducted wide propaganda on the Inter-State Succession Bill and the Marriage Bill. Mrs. Renuka Ray was nominated to the Central Legislative Assembly as a representative of the All India Women's Conference. Funds were collected by all the branches for relief work after Midnapur Cyclones in 1942. Lady Rama Rau collected a large sum of money for Bijapur famine relief operations. Lady Rama Rau also organized an exhibition of embroidery and needlework at the centre for the women of her district. The Standing committee at Khar demanded a revision of the Famine code in the light of the conditions at Bijapur. When Bengal was affected by a terrible famine in 1943, Smt. Vijaylakshmi Pandit and Mrs. Urmila Mehta toured the area, organized relief work and sent donations worth Rs. 60,000. A central fund, known as "Save the Children Fund," and later as 'All India Save the Children Committee', was also established. Its object was to save the destitute children of the famine affected area. When the Government enforcded a ban on women working in underground mines, it was the direct outcome of the demands made by AIWC.

In 1945, the Eighteenth session was held at Hyderabad, Sind. Smt. Hansa Mehta, the first women Vice-Chancellor of India, presided over it. As the World War II had ended, many delegates attended the session from foreign countries as well.

The Standing Committee was authorized to draft a Women's Charter to demand their rights as citizens of free India and a Memorandum embodying the concrete demands of the pan-Arabic Women's Association for rescinding the Balfour Declaration was prepared and accepted. During the year 1944, membership of the AIWC rose to 2500 in its 180 constituent branches divided into 41 branch areas. The Standing Committee appointed three members to give evidence before the Hindu Law Committee and to submit a Memorandum to the Government. The Conference also established an organization to begin an All India Milk Campaign for the health of children.

The Conference collected money for the Kasturba Memorial Fund and it opened twenty permanent Homes in Bengal, Orissa and Malabar to help orphans and destitutes. The progress of Lady Irwin College attracted the attention of the Government and it had to grant a sum of Rs. 10,000 to it. The Conference also supported the agitation of some servants of the State and against the death sentences passed on the Ashto and Chimur prisoners. The Central office and the branches extended their co-operation to the Planning Adviser of the Government of India in collecting data on the diet of pregnant mothers in India. Many branches of the Conference opened community kitchens, milk centres, industrial centres, fair price grain shops and co-operative stores. The President and the Secretary of the AIWC inspected the branches and gave fresh impetus to boost the all-round progress and development.

The nineteenth session was held at Akola in 1946 under the Presidentship of Lady Rama Rau. The record of work for the year 1945 revealed that many new branches had been opened. Mrs. Hansa Mehta was appointed a member to the UNO Sub-commission on the 'Status of Women' and subsequently she was appointed as the Indian representative on the Human Rights Commission of the UNO. Another woman leader, Begum Hamida Ali, represented India on the Status of Women Commission. Smt. Vijay Lakshmi Pandit was appointed leader of the Indian delegation to the General Assembly of the UNO and she fought successfully the case of Indians in South Africa. Rajkumari Amrit Kaur was elected as the Vice-President of UNESCO. The Conference of 1946 was attended by many distinguished foreign women. The Conference drafted a Charter on Women's Rights and Duties, and prepared a Memorandum on planning for National Welfare. It observed the All India Food Day and the AIWC Day. It conducted symposiums on the Education of Women in Modern India and on Juvenile Literature in India which were also published. Hajrah Begum translated two pamphlets in Hindustani on the Charter of Women's Rights and Duties and the Report of Tea Plantation Labour in Assam. Mrs. H. Selingam presented to the Conference the Asoka-Akbar Mobile Health Van to provide medical relief in isolated villages of India.

In 1947, the twentieth session of the Conference was held at Madras. Smt. Anusuiya Bai Kale was in the Chair. The report included the opening of three new main branches of the Conference raising the total membership to 3500. In the journal *Roshni*, Mrs. Pupul Jaykar published an article on the Indian Civil Code and Mrs. Avabai Wadia published 'Some Careers for Women'. All these tracts were expressions of their mental and intellectual calibre. The Conference sent twelve members to attend the Asian Relations Conference.

It was redeeming to note that the Social Council placed the All India Women's Conference on its list of Non-Governmental organizations having Consultative status. Under the direction of the well-known foreign educationist, Miss Mary Sweeny, a three months Pre-Basic Teacher Training Course was conducted through the Central office of the Conference. Thirty one specially selected women teachers from different parts of the country took advantage of this new scheme. A Nursery School was started to serve as the workshop of this Course. It was later handed over to the Bombay Mahila Sangh—a constituent branch of the Bombay All India Women's Conference.

The Conference made stupendous progress in various fields after the country attained independence. It conducted programme for relief and rehabilitation of the refugees. In Madras, Dr. Muthulakshmi led the campaign for providing X-ray apparatus for the treatment of Cancer. It began a vigorous propaganda for the Hindu Code Bill. The various branches extended active co-operation and full support for the implementation of the Five Year Plans. Many branches opened youth sections and other social, educational and medical centres for the social well-being. The Central Office of the Conference was shifted to New Delhi. The building was designed to serve as the memorial to two of the outstanding pioneer leaders, Smt. Sarojini Naidu and Margaret Cousins.

There were many other organizations which actively

conducted programmes to strengthen feminism in India. They made efforts "to provide numerous women with an opportunity for self-development and self-expression."

(a) The Hindu Women's Rescue Home Society

In the memory of Swami Shraddhananda, who died in 1927, an institution was started to provide shelter, relief and to render other assistance to women and children in distress without any distinction of colour, class or creed. It endeavoured to heal up the grave sores of the women who suffered at the hands of society, The fallen women, the deserted wife, the despised widow, the betrayed virgin, the neglected orphan and the unclaimed infants were protected properly. The Government later recognized this Home for the detention of conditionally released female convicts. The Home also made provision for education of the boys and girls and imparted training to grown up women in arts and crafts like sewing, embroidery, cutting and knitting, etc. It also made provisions for the training of nurses to work in the medical field.

(b) The Parsee Mahila Sangh

It catered to the needs of the women of Parsi families. It was started in 1934 and through it feminism and nationalism were promoted among women. It started several schools. It also protested against the prevalent social evils. It also worked to stop the traffic in female flesh. It tried to secure employment for the educated as well as uneducated women. It also formed a group of 'Sevikas' to serve the society during the period of natural calamities.

(c) Dayalbagh Mahila Association

It provided training to women with a view to make them

economically independent. Trained women taught the girls of Dayalbagh school, the art of embroidery and sewing. In 1938, the Dayalbagh Mahila co-operative Association was established at Agra in 1938. Its object was to attain the general well-being of women. The Association worked through a Managing Committee. It conducted the constructive work of various institutions for women. The Dayalbagh co-operative Mahila Tailoring School was established to provide two year's course in tailoring, embroidery, knitting, cut-work and toy-making. It also taught specialization in machine embroidery to the women of the Radhasoami Satsang, Dayalbagh. A Sewa Sangh was organized to look after the poor, needy and helpless old women. They started three well-equipped libraries for the children and a Store to sell the products of Dayalbagh Industries. The Mahila Association also provided its members with an opportunity to serve the Ayurvedic Pharmacy as helpers. The members prepared spices for Mahila Stores. They also set up refreshment stalls on occasions of Bhandaras (religious gatherings) and took active part in the annual sale of Dayalbagh goods through exhibitions. Through the Dayalbagh Marriage Panchayat Act, they succeeded in simplifying the marriage rules and reducing the marriage expenditures to the minimum.

(d) The Kasturba Trust

To commemorate Kasturba's name, the Kasturba Trust was founded for the uplift of rural women. Its object was to look after the general welfare of the poor and needy women and children of the villages. It concentrated its activities on education and medical aid. It trained women workers for conducting its programme of relief. Its branches were spread in different villages of the country. It tried to evoke the emotions of the people against the terrible consequences of abduction, and, finally, creating a sense of shame and guilt for such acts.

These Women's organizations truly represented the firm faith and determination of the Indian Women to march ahead on the path of peace, progress and prosperity. The women of India, strongly knit together as they were, made zealous efforts, no longer to put up with their degraded and depraved status in society. No wonder, that they began to express a remarkable readiness to face the hard realities of life and come out victorious in the long struggle. These organizations, spread almost all over India, fought for eradicating the social evils, as well as for attaining academic and technical education. The feminist movement in the country worked unabated and in a vigorous manner through these organizations which were in almost all big cities of India.

It is true that the most important of these organizations was the All India Women's Conference. The organization developed from its modest and restricted programme of growth and development of female education in the country to a full-fledged national institution embracing even global problems in its purview. In the beginning, this Conference achieved a great success in the field of education for women. It favoured such an education as would make the women fit to play their role in the family and train them in the principles of self-dependent citizenship. It favoured such a curriculum as might assist them to become wise citizens. It laid emphasis on the teacher's training schemes and education of adult women in the country.

In the social field, the Conference carried on effective propaganda against early marriage, polygamy, purdah and dowry. It supported widow-marriage and the property right for the women. It became responsible for the enforcement of progressive social legislations in the country. The aims and objects of the All India Women's Conference were quite broad and all embracing.

The work-programme of A.I.W.C. were the following:

1. To work actively for the general progress and welfare of women and children.
2. To inculcate in women and children, the ideal of true citizenship.
3. To promote education along right lines.
4. To work and press for social reforms.
5. To strive to establish equal rights and opportunities for all.
6. To work for a free and united India.
7. To set and demand a high moral standard in all departments of united India.
8. To demand for international goodwill and world peace.

It not only supported the social legislations but also prepared the ground for their enactment by creating a congenial atmosphere in the Assemblies and outside. It staunchly believed in the women's elevation through legislative measures. It demanded complete economic equality for work and wages in different vocations, such as nursing, teaching, etc. It pleaded with the government against the unhealthy working conditions of women labourers, their low wages and the absence of material and cultural facilities to the working class women. It also fought for the women working in the underground mines. It made suggestions to improve the efficiency and interest of women workers by giving them right to enter any profession or trade union, by providing residence to them when they were transferred, by guaranteeing them adequate basic wages and dearness allowance, by adhering to the policy of equal pay for equal work and by providing them maternity benefits, etc. It carried on a vehement propaganda against international traffic of women and children. It concentrated its efforts to stop the immoral practice of Devdasis in the country. It made a strong appeal to the Government not to enforce indiscriminately the existing laws against the dirty practice of traffic in women and to establish Government Rescue Homes for the so-called fallen and the destitute women.

Though the Conference did not act as a political organization, it fought for women's political rights as well. It demanded franchise for all women, married or unmarried and asserted that departments like Health, Education and Labour should be invariably given to women legislators. The members of the Conference who represented India in the various international organizations were able to depict an efficient picture of Indian womanhood before the world. It stressed on the utility of family planning and expressed its concern on the rapid growth of population in the country. It prepared a scheme for rural reconstruction and arranged for mobile dispensaries for medical relief. It published the journal *Roshni* regularly and also issued special bulletins and journals to popularize its programmes among the general public.

The Conference could draw to its fold only the upper middle class women of the society. Only a few of the upper middle class women held the leadership of the Conference. They could neither understand the problems of the women masses, nor could they do anything substantial to solve their problems. Their indifference towards the projects that could benefit the women masses was strange. No doubt, they passed resolutions after resolutions. The leaders did not take interest in the rural areas. The work of the Conference remained confined to the cities. Their high sounding resolutions for improving the working condition of women labourers remained merely a scrap on paper.

Due to the pressure of men reformers, the government had to enact legislations against Sati and infanticide. It had also enacted Widow Re-marriage Act in 1856. But during the period that followed the establishment of the All India

Women's Conference, the government had to change its rigid attitude towards social problems and adopt a liberal outlook. As a result the feminist movement found its rare expression in the country.

As early as 1890, due to the reform propaganda, the Indian Penal code had declared the consummation of the marriage at the age of ten. But the age of marriage was still very low. In 1890, the age of consent was raised to twelve years. But the law remained unknown to the vast majority and the evil of early marriage persisted in the country. In 1925, an Act was passed differentiating between marital and extra-marital sexual consummation. The All-India Women's Conference suggested amendments in Rai Sahab Har Bilas Sarda's Act and fully supported it. No Act could be enacted for equal wages to women workers with men workers before 1975. In the Women's year, the programmes of women's welfare were taken up on priority by the Government of free India. Yet some pockets remained untouched in the country.

The Conference did not remain inactive during the post freedom period. According to the Report of All-India Women's Conference "since independence we have become interested more in constructive work rather than the agitational attitude that we took in pre-independence era."

Most of the women leaders of A.I.W.C. were freedom fighters who played a distinctive role in winning over the sympathies of the rulers of the day. They carried sufficient weight by virtue of their meritorious position in life and the feelings that they had to serve the country. It was through them that the women of this country tasted the delicious fruits of social equality. They indeed attained a unique fulfilment in their mission.

7. In Politics

Prior to the 18th century renaissance, Indian women generally kept themselves away from politics, except those who belonged to the royal classes. They made a mark in war, diplomacy and administration. Rani Kaikeyi of the epic age became famous for her tact and bravery. The medieval period produced some outstanding women administrators and rulers like Rani Rudradama of Warangal, Razia Sultana, Rani Durgawati of Gondwana, Chandbibi of Ahmadnagar, Nur Jahan, Tarabai, and Ahalya Bai Holkar. During the British period, Rani of Jhansi emerged as a great heroine of the Revolt of 1857. Her bravery and courage were exemplary. When Jhansi was annexed by the British, the Rani submitted a petition of protest to the government of Great Britain. She boldly declared that the people of Jhansi did not wish to be the subjects of the East India Company. The Rani along with the people, fought valiantly against the English army and preferred death rather than falling in the hands of the enemy.

Other prominent women who participated in the armed resistance of 1857 were Rani Tace Bai, Begum Hazrat Mahal, Lalita Bakhshi, Jhalkari, Sunder, Kashi Bai, Moti Bai, Rani of Ramgarh and Rani of Tulsipur. They were, indeed, gallant fighters of freedom. Their exemplary courage, integrity, self-respect combined with the spirit of sacrifice, dedication and devotion to motherland, made them the champions of freedom. Though very few in number, they symbolized a bunch of fresh flowers full of fragrance of bravery and beauty along with womanly merits of the Vedic Indian. The twentieth century Indian women were so patriotic that they entered into politics in large numbers. They bravely participated in the national struggle. The Women's Suffrage Movement began in India as early as 1917. It was through this movement that women leaders made efforts for advancement of women in general. The Indians began to realize that if the feminist movement succeeds, it would prove to be the key to the freedom of the country.

The reformers of the country also felt that India would not achieve the position which it aspires until its women play a constructive role in the national movement. The Federation of University Women in India, composed of various associations of women graduates, was established to promote the Indian women's interest in the national struggle. M.E. Cousins writes that, "I had been only a year in the country but I felt within myself that unless the Indian women jump into politics, nothing solid could be achieved. My husband and me read the newspaper that a never-ending stream of men are going in deputation to the Viceroy and the Secretary of State, Montague. They never mentioned the voice of the Indian women. All my training in organizing, in taking hold of psychological moments, could not be curbed. I approached about 20 of India's best known women in public life, most of whom I had met through the Senate Meeting of Prof. Karve's Indian Women's University. Eventually it became my privilege to organize and carry through the one and only women's deputation calling for Indian constitutional reforms. In fact, how the women's deputation came to include political demands in its Memorandum is an interesting story."

Mrs. Cousins further narrates the historic turn and writes that, "In the middle of October 1917, after much wiring and writing, I got an application or a deputation signed by a number of leading women belonging to various parts of India and sent it to the organizers of the Montague Chelmsford team. Then came an interesting turn of events which indicated that something in the cosmos had a bigger plan of the immediate future of Indian womanhood. Our application which was for an opportunity to state the claim for the extension of girl's education, was declined as being out side the terms of enquiry which was limited to purely political considerations.... There was no alternative to the direction of fate.... Again wires and letters, anticipations, 'stone walls' and jungles of discouragement so dark that you could not see either the wood or the trees, rays of heart lifting light, refusals, promises and, at last, on November 28 (1917) a wire saying that a deputation of ladies on the subject of Women's suffrage would be received." ... Mrs. Sarojini Naidu was the spokeswoman of the 14 women stalwarts who called upon the Viceroy and Mr. Montague in Madras city on 19th December 1917.

These women organized various public meetings in support of Women's Suffrage held mainly by the various branches of the Women's Indian Association in favour of their own claim. They also organized local political conferences to propagate their cause. The Muslim League and the Indian National Congress in their sessions supported their demands. Another deputation of women waited on the Southborough Commission on Franchise Reform, which gave the first rebuff to the cause in 1918. With undaunted courage and fresh aspirations, the women leaders sent another deputation to the Joint Parliamentary Committee on the Government of India Bill of 1919.

Mrs. Annie Besant, Mrs. Sarojini Naidu, Mrs. Herabai Tata, and Miss Mithan Tata, Bar-at-Law, were so convincing in their arguments that the British Parliament decided to consider votes for Indian Women a 'Domestic Subject', which Indian Provincial Legislatures might settle for themselves, the official Government members being left free to vote as they liked. This course of action proved the 'open sesame' of citizenship to Indian womanhood. The British Parliament, perhaps, did not expect such a revolutionary step from the conservative Indians and it was astonishing for them to find that the Indian legislatures, one after another, enfranchised their women on the same terms as men. In granting women suffrage, Indian men showed great statesmanship, understanding of democratic values, sympathetic vision of the aspirations of the women, and courage to take a great progressive step.

The most striking aspect of the movement was the help and co-operation extended by men legislators to the efforts of the women leaders. Dewan Bahadur M. Krishnan Nair moved the resolution on Women's franchise in the Madras Legislative Council in 1921, providing it the honour of being the first legislature in the whole of India to grant the right of vote to the women. When the Women's Indian Association felicitated him at a meeting, he said that, "the cause of the women's franchise was so strong, just and good that it was bound to succeed and that the attitude of the Council was on the whole very sympathetic."

In 1923, the Legislative Council of the United Provinces granted Women's Suffrage. The women of Assam, Burma and the Punjab including Delhi were also granted the right to vote at par with men by their Councils. In Bengal, the Women's Suffrage Movement succeeded in reversing its former defeat when enthusiastic leaders like Mrs. Sarla Devi Choudhrani and Mrs. Kumudini Basu supported it. On 16th August 1925 the Bengal Council passed the Women Franchise Resolution by a majority vote. The Central Provinces gave women the right to vote and the right to sit in the Councils by the same resolution in March 1927.

In the Bombay Presidency, the resolution for extension of the Legislative votes to women was debated at three sittings of the Council before finally passing it. Mrs. Ramabai Ranade was overwhelmed at the co-operation extended by men and other members of the council to her resolution in the Council. It was a strange phenomenon that support to the women's cause came from all communities in Bombay and it led to communal unity among the women in the province.

The Legislative council of Bihar and Orissa granted franchise to women in 1929 and completed the enfranchisement of the women of British India on the same terms as men. Various congratulatory messages were received from all over the world by the Women's Indian Association after the victory in Women's Suffrage Movement. Women went a step further and they expressed their resentment against the rules of Reform Act which prevented women from being eligible for either election or nomination to the Provincial Legislative Councils or the Imperial Legislatures.

A large meeting was held at the Senate House of Madras University under the joint auspices of the Women's Indian Association and the Bharat Stree Mahamandal, the Women Graduates Union, the Stree Sharda Union, the Madras Branch of Brahmo Samaj and the Tamilian Ladies Association, to express resentment over the disqualification of their sex from entering the Legislatures. Another representative meeting of women was held at Bombay at the Marwari Vidyalaya under the joint auspices of the Women's Indian Association, the Gujrati Hindu Stree Mandal, the Bombay Presidency Women Graduates' Union, the Stree Jain Mahila Samaj, the Pathare Prabhu Mahila Samaj and Bhagini Samaj. Lady Dhunbai Cowasji Jehangir was the Chair Person of this meeting.

They passed a resolution requesting the Governor to recommend to the Viceroy and the Secretary of State for India, to revise the Rules of the Reform Act which disqualified women from membership of the Legislative and Imperial Councils and to amend them so as to enable the women to become members of the Council. In 1924, a meeting of Indian women belonging to different parts of the county was held at Simla for revision of its clauses. The efforts of Mrs. Cousins, Herabai Tata, Mrs. Faridoonji and many known and unknown enlightened women became successful and the government amended the Bill accordingly. Women got the right to sit in Legislative Councils of Madras, Bombay, the Punjab and the Central Provinces in April 1926 in pursuance of the Minutes of the Meeting held on March 13, 1924. The first two women to contest the elections to the Legislative Council were Mrs. Kamladevi Chattopadhyaya and Mrs. Hannah Angelo—the Secretary of the Nurses' Association, Madras.

The first woman doctor, Punnen Lukose, M.L.C., was chosen in Travancore to act as Minister of Health and her work was highly applauded. Mrs. Madhavi Amma of Trichur was nominated as a member of Cochin Legislative Council. There she unhesitatingly expressed her views on the subjects concerning the welfare of women and children. It was an event of great success for the women when in 1927 the Governor of Madras nominated Dr. Muthulakshmi Ammal, a well-known medical practitioner to be the member of Madras Legislative Council. It took not more than twenty years, that the women of India passed from apathetic indifference to eager activity and an acute awareness of their responsibility as active citizens. They became conscious of the claims of the national life and with breathe-taking abruptness they jumped into the national struggle and began dominating the political life of the country.

Women continued their agitation through the All-India Women's Conference safeguarding their special interests vis a-vis the Reform Bill and the proposed Constitution of 1935. They waited in the deputation on the Viceroy for pressing the inclusion of women delegates to the Round Table Conference. Indian women opposed communal electorates, reservation of seats for women and wife-hood qualification. They demanded equality with men and requested for the adult suffrage for women. The All India Women's Conference did commendable services to support these reforms.

Women joined the national movement in large numbers and displayed their heroic talents. When the Indian National Congress was founded in 1885, the women of India were passing through the process of social transition. A.O. Hume, while laying its foundation did not forget to add that, "the political reformers of all shades of opinion should never forget to add that unless the elevation of female element of the nation proceeds with equal pace, all their labour for the political enfranchisement will prove in vain." Women did not come forward to participate in the Congress programmes till the session of 1900. The first woman to speak from the Congress stage was Smt. Swarna Kumari Devi and she attended the session the same year with Mrs. K. Ganguli and a few other educated women.

Women discarded seclusion and came out to attend the Congress sessions in large numbers. The feminist movement was developing fast in the country and an all round awakening among them began to manifest itself with concrete results. People thought it better to channelize the spirit of feminism to nationalism which was the need of the hour. It was Gandhiji, who spoke publicly about the latent qualities and spiritual fervour with moral capabilities. Gandhiji emerged on the Indian political scene in 1918 after closely watching the political events in the country for nearly three years. He adopted the new technique of passive resistance or Satyagraha to attain freedom. In his opinion, women were the most suited to discreetly use the new weapons of non-violence and truth.

The enlightened Indian women themselves thought that the help and co-operation extended to the British during the first Great War would not go without results. Some of them collected war-funds and many others had taken jobs in order to be helpful to the British in the hour of their need. Many had lost their fathers, husbands and sons who were serving in the British army and had gone abroad to fight for the alien rulers. The women knew that the situation demanded greater sacrifices from them. Instead of granting political relief to the people of India, the British Government enacted the Rowlatt Bill in 1919, increased the prices heavily, proclaimed Martial Law, and became responsible for the grim tragedy of the Jallianwala Bagh in Punjab. Gandhiji moved a resolution of pursuing the policy of progressive non-violence and non-cooperation until the wrongs were undone and Swarajya was attained. It was ratified with a thumping majority.

The women of India had earlier demonstrated their strength against the partition of Bengal in 1905. They observed Raksha Bandhan and exhorted the men to take up the task of Bengal's unity. They also donated generously in cash and kind for the national struggle. When Gandhiji gave a clarion call to women, they were fully prepared to jump into the national movement and join their men-folk. They struggled through all crisis and danger. The narrow domestic walls gave way to a broader human relationship of the new setting in which they were accorded a position of honour. Adhering to the creed of non-violence, they formed the organization of Desh-Sewikas and marched ahead towards the goal. They collected funds for the national movement and even offered their own ornaments for the purpose. They picketed the foreign shops, educational institutions, the Courts, the Legislatures and Stores dealing in liquor and foreign goods.

They burnt "holi" of their costly costumes manufactured in foreign mills. They boldly withstood the trials at the courts, suffered lathi charges and imprisonment. They showed remarkable capacity to bear tortures and pain. They participated in the no-tax campaign of Bardoli, and took the pledge to remain non-violent under all circumstances. They joined the famous Dandi March of Gandhiji in 1930, who had made special appeals to them through his "Young India" to take up Charkha and start spinning. He further exhorted them to stick to picketing the shops of foreign goods. The call had a miraculous effect and thousands of women, even from the aristocratic families, gladly offered themselves to the cause of the country. They became active members of the Satyagraha movement and faced arrests, insults and beatings.

M. Cousins writes: "The response to the call of Mahatma Gandhi was magnificent. Within the next three years over five thousand women had served the terms of severe imprisonment, suffered lathi charges, loss of property, caste, health, livelihood and reputation. They willingly faced publicity of the most trying kind...". They sacrificed all kinds of cherished privileges of caste, ceremonial purity and privacy. The Indian League Delegation declared in 1932 that—

> "the worst cases of ill treatment of women and children have occurred. Most of the excesses and atrocities occurred in the villages and inside the prisons.... In many instances of which we have the facts, women were savagely set upon, beaten or insulted by the police with the object of preventing them from participating in the movement conducted by Indian National Congress under the leadership of Gandhiji."

The participation of women not only increased the numerical strength of the freedom fighters but also enhanced the moral force of their men encouraging them to perform greater service and sacrifices for the country. Many leaders like Sarojini Naidu came forward to offer their services to the difficult ventures of individual Satyagraha. The women adopted the programme of *Swaraj, Swadeshi* and *Shiksha*. They shared these efforts through Press and platform. Mrs. Macdonald who visited India during the period observed that "there was a tremendous movement going on amongst the Indian women...".

In the words of Valentine Chirol, "The revolt seems to have obtained a firm-hold of the Zenana." In fact, the women led processions, organized meetings, sang national songs, spun Churkha and spread the fire of political self-consciousness. They had to face filthy language and threats of dishonour either expressed or thinly veiled. The Desh Sevikas joined the ceremonies of flag salutation and march-past. They actively participated in organizing Hartals. They also cooked food for the wounded and nursed them. Many of them sold 'Khaddar' and also regularly wore it. They travelled far and wide to spread the message of Mahatma Gandhi. In spite of the police action, they remained firm and unyielding. The Britishers were amazed and stunned to see their performance.

The Indian women earned great admiration from all corners of the world. Mrs. Gray observed in 1932: "If the women are to be judged by deeds rather than by words it is within the Congress that they have shown the greatest courage."... They have picketed, walked in processions, have gone to prison and have proved their courage in many a dangerous riots. The ill-treatment of women by the police surpassed all sense of decorum and decency. They were made to travel alone to far off places; separated from their little children and family members and were beaten mercilessly. They were compelled to live under male custody as prisoners. They became victims of merciless behaviour, rape and indecent assaults.

In Borsad, the women were dispersed by force and when they were thrown down, the police trampled them. In 1942, during the Quit India Movement, women had to direct the national movement, for many of the men-workers and leaders had been sent behind the bars a day earlier. Women organized the political prisoners Relief Fund and were able to collect large sums of money for the purpose. They organized camps to train women workers. They were also taught lathi-drill and sword-play. In the hour of great crisis and uncertainty, women succeeded in their sublime mission of freedom of their country.

Indian women's unbounded passion for liberty and their capacity for self-sacrifice, indeed proved their worth and quality. They continued to participate in the political struggle right up to 1947, when the country attained freedom from the alien rule. They were dragged by hair, their saris were torn, and they were abused indecently. Their belongings and property were wantonly destroyed. They, indeed, stood gallantly, shoulder to shoulder with men-folk in the front line of India's National Army and truly shared the trials and tribulations of the national struggle. Extremely able and patriotic women members of the Congress made the cause of freedom of the country an essential part of their personal programme.

In 1906, Mrs. Sarojini Bose pledged in the provincial Conference that she would not put on gold bangles until the Bande Matram circular prohibiting the use of slogans was cancelled. Sushila Devi of Sialkot attacked the government and vehemently demonstrated through a procession and exhorted the women to rise to the occasion. Smt. Purani Devi—an Arya Samaj worker of Hissar, toured the various districts of Punjab and advocated the cause of Swadeshi. Agyawati, who belonged to Delhi propagated the awakening of women and urged their participation in the country's mission. She started a Widow's Home for training women in various crafts and useful activities. Mrs. Radhe Devi, wife of Lala Lajpat Rai, delivered a lecture at the meeting of Punjab Congress that the object was to strike a note of warning to the inactive men. Parvati Bai was an ardent Congress worker who went to jail several times. She was sentenced to two years rigorous imprisonment for her 'inflaming speech'. Bee Amman was an aristocratic Muslim lady who discarded Purdah and addressed meetings all over India. She advocated Hindu-Muslim Unity and the use of Khaddar. She worked in the Khilafat Movement also. She exhorted on the women to use their spiritual power and help their men to tread the right path. Among the foreign women working in India, Sister Nivedita had full sympathy with the cause of freedom. In 1904, she condemned the Convocation speech of Lord Curzon at Calcutta University. She propagated the use of Swadeshi goods and inspired the women to take to Charkha and other crafts. She criticized the education policy of the government and the sad affairs in agriculture.

The promotion of the cause of Indian nationalism along with the progress of female education was the mission of her life. She wrote: "We had been sacrificing ourselves, for our fathers and husbands and sons, but so long as this spirit of Indian womanhood is not lost, I for one feel that we must now sacrifice for the motherland." Smt. Basanti Devi and Urmila Devi, went about the streets of Calcutta, propagating the use of Khadi and preaching against intemperance. They were arrested while selling handloom cloth. Smt. Anukul Mitter, Smt. Surya Shome, Smt. Umashi Devi, Smt. Satya Devi and eight Sikh ladies were also arrested along with them. Urmila Devi urged women to join the ranks of volunteers. Mrs. Basanti Devi presided over the Bengal Provincial Congress Session in 1922 at Chittagong. She said: "Freedom will come as a matter of course to the extent we are able to do penance by our sacrifices, by our sorrows and sufferings." Sarla Devi, the great champion of women's movement, was a great patriot. She guided the activities of the *Samitis* and trained its members through religious ceremonies, by delivering inflammatory speeches, quoting revolutionary literature and through participation in political meetings and making demonstrations. Her fiery speeches filled the people with the hope of a new resurgence. She later became a follower of Gandhiji and participated in the Civil Disobedience Movement.

Kasturba Gandhi, the devoted wife of Gandhiji, represented the innate piety of Indian womanhood. She started her political activities in South Africa. She entered the area of Transvaal without permit along with sixteen other women. She was sentenced to three months rigorous imprisonment. Gandhiji was arrested in 1922 and Kasturba inspired the workers to continue the struggle. When she presided over the Gujarat Provincial Conference, she condemned untouchability and advised women to take up the use of Swadeshi. She was, in fact, a valiant participator in the freedom struggle which her great husband led. Swaroop Rani Nehru, the wife of Motilal Nehru, took part in the Civil Disobedience Movement. While leading the procession, she received a severe lathi blow and became unconscious. Kamla Nehru, the young wife of Jawahar Lal, had to bear separation from her husband—who was imprisoned many a times for his activities in the National Movement. Kamla also led processions and organized the work of U.P. Congress Committee with great zeal and fervour at Allahabad. Mrs. Vijay Lakshmi Pandit visited many countries of the world and spoke on India's problems to create sympathy in their hearts for the National Movement. She was a stalwart among the women leaders of Uttar Pradesh. Defying the police orders, she held the meeting of the District Conference of the Congress near the clock-tower at Allahabad. She was arrested and sentenced to one year's rigorous imprisonment. Mrs. Uma Nehru and Smt. Rameshwari Nehru also worked in the Satyagraha movement. Chandrawati Lakhanpal went from village to village and organized the villagers to fight for the national cause. She was arrested in 1932 and sentenced to one year's imprisonment.

Other prominent women leaders were Mrs. Annie Besant, Mrs. Sarojini Naidu, Rajkumari Amrit Kaur, and Durgabai Deshmukh. Mrs. Annie Besant asserted, that "India must be governed on the basis of Indian feelings, Indian traditions, Indian thoughts and Indian ideas." She delivered a series of lectures to mark the beginning of an earnest and concerted movement for self-government in India. According to her, self-government was not a reward for India but it was a right. To achieve the goal with law-abiding and constitutional methods, she founded the Home Rule League. The Government fined her for and banned her journals. Her entry in the Bombay Presidency was banned. When she was imprisoned in 1917, protest meetings and demonstrations were held all over the country. Along with Tilak, she submitted a memorandum to Mr. Montague on 26th November 1917 which covered a joint deputation of the League and the Congress. As Congress President, she delivered a forceful speech which was rightly acclaimed as the 'Magna Carta of India's liberty'. She did not agree with the Reform Bill of 1919. She protested against the Simon Commission and propagated in favour of Nehru Report. It was she who inspired women to join politics and participate in the National Movement.

Sarojini Naidu was a staunch supporter of Hindu-Muslim unity. She said in 1909, "The highest ideal, the climax of modern spirit has been unity." She organized demonstrations against the Rowlatt Act and protested against the Act of 1919. She was elected to the office of Congress President in 1925. She renounced her title of Kaiser-i-Hind to the British government in protest against the British apathy towards Indians. She was incharge of Dharsana Salt raid in 1930. She exhorted upon women to join the national movement. She was imprisoned many a times for her patriotic activities.

Kamla Devi Chattopadhyaya was a reputed leader who threw herself whole-heartedly into the political struggle of

India. For participating actively in the Non-cooperation programme, she was imprisoned by the government. Later, Kamla Devi became one of the organizer-founders of the All-India Congress Socialist Party. She visited Europe and America and exchanged ideas with the leaders of the Western world. A gifted writer, she wrote many essays and books. Mrs. Lado Rani Zutshi, Parbati Bai, Smt. Kartar Kaur and Atma Devi, all were famous for picketing the shops of foreign goods and the law courts. Rukmini Lakshmipati participated in the Salt Satyagraha. She was the President of Tamil Nadu Provincial Congress Committee. Durgabai Deshmukh was appointed dictator in the Salt Satyagraha of 1930-31 and was arrested. Besides the celebrated Annie Besant, another notable Irish woman who took keen interest in the Indian National Movement was Margaret Cousins. In 1932, she went to America and delivered lectures against the imprisonment of Mahatma Gandhi, Kasturba and Sarojini Naidu. She organized meetings in India to keep the British Government under pressure.

Kanaklata Barua marched in a procession to occupy the government buildings in Assam. In spite of the warnings of the police inspector, she did not move. She was shot in the chest. Bhogeswar Phoo Kanan was also shot for holding the tricolour flag. Smt. Annupriya Barua and Sudhalata Dutta, encouraged the people and organized the Red Cross First Aid Society. They distributed warm clothes, bandage and other amenities to the workers of Assam. Mrs. Anna Prava Barua had to bear police tortures for two long years because her husband was a great revolutionary fighter for India's freedom.

Chandra Prabha Saikani and Sita Bhuwaneshwari Devi organized Kirtans, requested the police men to resign from their posts and secretly celebrated freedom day. These ladies were, therefore, brutally assaulted. Rajkumari Amrit Kaur took active part in the Salt campaign. When Communal

Award was announced, she protested against it and moved a resolution at a meeting of All India Women's Conference. In protest, she actively participated in the movement of 1942. She was subjected to a severe lathi charge in Simla, while she was leading a procession. She was arrested at Kalka. The cell in which she was kept was filthy and unhygienic. Man Mohini Sehgal, Parvati Devi, Lakshmi Devi, Amar Kaur and Pushpa Gujral were also women freedom fighters. They raised the banner of patriotism high in Punjab. Anusuyabai Kale was a prominent leader of M.P. She took active part in the Civil Disobedience Movement of 1930 and suffered imprisonment. She participated in the struggle of 1942. In Bengal, Lotika Ghosh formed Mahila Rashtriya Sangha. The organization sent batches for nearly six months for picketing and courting arrests. They picketed schools and colleges also. Arunbala Sen was an active member of the revolutionary organization. Nari Satyagraha Committees were founded by Urmila Devi to take out processions in violation of government orders. Other active members were Mohini Devi, Jyotirmoyi Ganguli, Hem Prabha Das Gupta, Ashoklata Das, Sumiti Das and Bimal Prativa Devi.

Ladies Picketing Board was started to conduct programmes of boycott and picketing in collaboration with the Bengal Provincial Congress Committee. The organization worked under different sections such as—(1) Boycott and Picketing Section for peaceful picketing programme; (2) Swadeshi Prachar Section for preaching the use of Khadi and to recruit women to join the board; (3) Prabhat Pheri Section to take out processions; (4) Constructive Worker Section to give demonstration in the use of Charkha and Takli and to help spinners to get in touch with markets for the yarn spun by them; (5) The General Section to hold meetings and decide future course of action. The organization urged the need for the formation of Mahila Samitis, for boycotting foreign goods, for establishing Hindu-Muslim unity and for removing purdah and untouchability. It also demanded open trial for men who were political prisoners and were still rotting in jails.

Many others in Bombay took part in the national movement. Jaishree Raiji, Hansa Mehta, Perin Captain, Sofia Somjee, Lilavati Munshi, Maniben Patel and Khurshedben boldly participated in the political struggle. In the movement of 1942, Mrs. Sucheta Kripalani, Tarkeshwari Sinha, Aruna Asaf Ali, Rajendra Kumari Bajpai, Nandini Satpathi, Begum Attia Habibullah and Mrs. Indira Gandhi played important roles. They led processions, addressed meetings and suffered imprisonments. Mrs. Ammu Swaminathan was a champion of Swadeshi who suffered imprisonment for participating in the Satyagraha movement. Mrs. Rukmani Lakshmipathi was the first woman prisoner in the Salt Satyagraha in the whole of India. She had joined the Congress along with her husband very early and had become a staunch worker. As men realized the inefficiency of the constitutional methods to win Swaraj, so did the daring among the women of India. Fed up with the slow and slack policy of the British Government and enraged with their repressive measures, many women came forward to show their capabilities as successful revolutionaries.

Mrs. S.K. Verma, Miss P. Nauroji and Madam B.K. Cama were among those women revolutionaries who worked outside India for the cause of India's freedom. Madam Cama left India in 1902 and toured Germany, Scotland and Paris. She settled down in London in 1906 where she met Shyamji Krishna Verma, an eminent Arya Samajist leader. In 1907, she attended the International Socialist Congress and spoke about the terrible tyrannies that the Indians were facing at the hands of British Government. She also delineated the causes and consequences of the exploitation done by the English capitalists. She developed contacts with nationalists in Ireland, Russia, Egypt and Germany. In 1908, she made a historic speech at India House, London, which inaugurated the basic programme of India's revolutionary party. Madam Cama used to supply arms packed in toys as gifts to the revolutionaries in India. She also sent them the revolutionary literature in the form of leaflets and financially helped them. She established her own Press from where she published a journal named 'Bande Matram'. She was convinced that the success in social and political field would not be complete, unless women came forward to become active participants in the country's struggle. Great and gallant as she was, she soon became widely known all over the world.

Inheriting in her blood the spark of patriotic fervour, Kumudani Mitter organized a revolutionary group. She helped the revolutionaries by maintaining contacts between the different underground leaders for whom the police was anxiously searching. She along with other members circulated revolutionary literature. She contributed thought-provoking articles in the magazine, *Suprabhat*—an important mouthpiece of the cult of revolution with the motto that "Motherland needed Blood." Revolutionary activities suited the emotionally strong Bengali women. The revolutionary organizations began to work in which young college girls had also joined with zeal and enthusiasm.

Kalpana Datta was one such girl who hated the Britishers. She joined the Calcutta University and took keen interest in the activities of the Ladies Club. She practised Lathi and did sword exercises. Later she joined the Dacca University and began to take part in the secret clubs which trained youngmen and women in the use of arms. Kalpana dressed up in male attire and raided the government buildings. Once she was arrested, but she ran away from the prison. She was re-arrested and sent before a special tribunal for the Chittagong Armoury Supplementary trials. She was sentenced to life transportation. Along with Kalpana, many young girls joined the secret activities of the revolutionary party. They raided the Railway Officers' Club at Pahartali in which a European lady was shot dead. Apprehending inevitable danger, the revolutionaries took potassium cyanide and died. Young and energetic, Suniti and Sumati were shot dead by the magistrate of Comilla in 1931.

There were many other girls who were very active. After their arrest, they admitted their offences declaring that love of Motherland prompted them to do so. They were sentenced to nine year's rigorous imprisonment. Along with her daughter, Mrs. B.C. Gupta of Mymensingh district was arrested for keeping three coils of fuse wire, seventy eight packets marked dynamite and lot of revolutionary literature.

Other prominent women revolutionaries of Bengal were Kamla Chatterjee, Bimal Pratibha, Shobaran Dutta, Ujjalla Devi, Parul Mukerjee, Joyti Kanti Dutta, Banlata Das and Shanti Ghose. Satyawati joined the Congress in 1930 and actively participated in picketing and processions as she was a revolutionary of high order. She distributed revolutionary literature and was twice tried for sedition. She contracted tuberculosis and died in 1946 declaring that her only desire was India's freedom. Usha Mehta started a Secret Radio—'Voice of Freedom'. Her Radio station, which she shifted from place to place had its own transmitter, recording station, call sign and a distinct wave length. Its first broadcast came on 14th August 1942. She herself broadcast fiery speeches on India's freedom struggle. She was ultimately arrested by the police. The idea of personal freedom ultimately created in them an interest in broader fields of life, such as, education and politics.

In the beginning, Indian politics was limited to the urban areas and to the educated classes. In other words, it was among a minority only. It was more of a class-movement than a mass-movement. Yet, the entry of women into politics was most remarkable, being so sudden and rather spectacular. The demand for equal right came from such women as were in contact with Western thought and ideals. They desired to be placed on an equal footing with their sisters in the West. Most surprising is the fact that the women's right to enfranchisement was scarcely questioned by men with whom lay the power to grant or refuse it. O'Malley writes, "Prima facie, their consent to such an innovation was an extra-ordinary concession, considering the almost ingrained view of the subordinate position of women and of their proper functions in life. The politically minded class has, however, always shown a singular facility for adopting the latest and most advanced political theories of the west, and, in addition to this, there was the ambition to keep pace with Western countries on the path of progress and to vindicate India in the eyes of the Western World ." There is, however, no denying to the fact that the women of India acquired equality and freedom almost as a free gift, a right which women of great Britain gained after years of struggle and agitation.

The greatest impetus, in fact, came from the clarion call of Mahatma Gandhi. Women living in Purda discarded it over-night and became ardent nationalists. They not only condemned their own inaction but also stirred up their menfolk into action. O'Malley rightly observes, "The call of Gandhi for active support from women in his campaign appealed at once to their sense of nationalism and to the spirit of selfless devotion which is characteristic of Indian womanhood.... They came out of purdah in thousands, and thousands have remained out of it.... There are great public gatherings of emancipated women which would have been unthinkable twenty years ago." The women of India felt that they had a special part to play in the national movement. Feminism and nationalism went hand in hand. One time a class movement, it assumed the shape of a mass-movement in which women occupied a prominent place. The world witnessed women standing shoulder to shoulder with men in the struggle for Indian liberation from foreign yoke.

The result of all this sudden and incessant political activity was that it unfolded the latent capacity of leadership in Indian women. They smilingly suffered inhuman tortures at the hands of the British officers and presented an unparalleled example of courage and heroism. The world was amazed at their inexhaustible capacity to suffer silently and work incessantly for the cause of the nation. They stood firm on the bedrock of patriotism. Nothing would misguide them or deter them from their path of service and sacrifice—not even the severe beatings dragging by hair or killing their innocent children before their eyes. Ultimately, the British officials were undoubtedly moved by the spirit of sacrifice and dedication of Indian womanhood. The women revolutionaries could be placed among the most daring women of the world. Their devotion to the cause of Motherland was surprisingly immense. Mother India would ever remember her illustrious daughters who willingly suffered privations and gladly embraced death so that their country might live long as a free and independent country.

8. Education and Career

Women's role in education and career in India was limited to a microscopic minority. Only some aristocratic Indian families, particularly those who belonged to the ruling classes, imparted education to their daughters. The British government remained apathetic to the problem of education, in general. In the 19th century, an official survey, conducted in different parts of the country revealed the fact that in Madras, only five thousand girls attended the indigenous primary schools against 1,78,630 boys. In Bombay, no girls were reported to be attending the school, but the girls in the upper class families received a little education at home. About the condition of female education in Bengal, Adam's report in 1835 says that the notion of providing the means of instruction for female children, never enters into the minds of parents. A superstitious feeling existed among majority of the Hindus, which was "principally cherished by the women and not discouraged by men, that a girl taught to write and read will, soon after marriage, become a widow." In Punjab, the picture of female education was somewhat encouraging. It was reported in 1849 that "female education is relished in all parts." Yet, the majority of women were not allowed the opportunity of education and development.

A few illustrious women, however, made their mark as statesmen, rulers, soldiers and saints. These, however, were exceptions. They did not reduce the gloom of the general picture of the subjection of women who were denied all opportunities for education, self-development and refinement.

The First Phase (1813-1854)

The East India Company was first obliged to accept the responsibility for the education of Indian people under the Charter Act of 1813. The Company officials, while working on the directive of the Parliament, restricted their educational activities to men and refused to take any direct action on the question of female education. They argued that the policy of the Company was one of strict social and religious neutrality; that the strong prejudices against female education were so deep rooted in the minds of the people that any attempt to educate women was sure to create a very great commotion. The first attempts of the Company should be restricted to the education of men, who might themselves at a later date, undertake the education of their womenfolk. They also refused to grant any freedom to them. Many men who received English education and admired Western culture, instructed their wives at home by Zanana teachers.

No financial assistance was given to special private schools established for girls in the country. The Indian private efforts were almost exclusively meant for boys and so were the private educational institutions of the missionary institutions. As such, the missionaries could not be an effective agency for the spread of education among Indian women. A splendid lead was given at this juncture by liberal Englishmen who realized that the education of women in India would develop, if the Indians cherished so. Among them may be mentioned the name of David Hare, who established a school for girls in Calcutta at his own expense. Professor Patton of the Elephantine Students Literary and Scientific Society established a number of girls' schools in the

City of Calcutta. J.E.D. Bethune, a member of the Council of Education in Bengal, established a girls' school at Calcutta and maintained it from his own funds till his death in 1851.

The missionaries and philanthropic Englishmen were making small efforts to educate girls. They wanted to break down the traditional popular resistance against the education of women. Raja Rammohun Roy, besides his campaign for the abolition of Sati and his vindication of women's right to property, emphatically asserted the need for female education. Pandit Ishwar Chandra Vidya Sagar, a great champion of women's education, was responsible for the establishment of a number of girls' school in Bengal. The Gujarat Vernacular society established a girls' school at Ahmedabad in 1849. Maganbhai Karamchand donated a large sum for starting girls' school in Gujarat. At Agra, Gopal Singh worked hard for the spread of literacy among women and conducted two hundred Seminars which no less than 3,800 girls had attended. Gopal Singh was the Deputy Inspector of Schools. He worked single handed and founded a large number of schools for girls. He could convince the government about the utility of female education and of the necessity of extending patronage to the girls' schools.

In other parts of the country also, Indians were establishing a number of special schools for girls with the help of liberal donations from the public. A vigorous propaganda was started through books, periodicals and lectures to persuade the people to give education to female members of their families. Lord Dalhousie observed on women's education in India in 1850 that "no single change in the habits of the people is likely to lead to more important and beneficial consequences than the introduction of education for their female children." He was of the opinion that a great work had been done for the successful introduction of native female education in India on a sound and solid foundation and that a stage had been reached when

Government should lend its "frank and cordial support" to the education of Indian women. The Court of Directors on the basis of above observation issued the Educational Despatch of 1854. The Despatch found that in spite of the lack of support from the State, 265 girls' schools with a total enrolment of about 8,000 of whom 1,110 were in Boarding schools, existed in Madras. In Bombay, there were 65 girls schools with an enrolment of about 6,500 pupils. In Bengal, it recorded the existence of 288 schools for girls with an enrolment of 6,869 pupils. In the North Western Provinces of Agra and Oudh, the Despatch found only 17 girls' schools with 386 pupils—all conducted by the Mission. In Punjab, the traditional institutions continued their efforts in the direction of female education and the modern type of schools had just begun to come into existence. Though not a very bright picture by any means, it offered a great contrast to the conditions that had existed in the early nineteenth century.

The Wood's Despatch stated: "The importance of female education in India cannot be over-rated and we have observed with pleasure the evidence which is now afforded of an increased desire on the part of many of the natives of India to give a good education to their daughters. By this means, a far greater proportional impulse is imparted to the educational and moral tone of the people than by the education of men. We have already observed that schools for females are included among those to which grants-in-aid may be given, and expressing our cordial sympathy with the efforts which are being made in this direction." Unfortunately, the enthusiasm with which the Despatch of 1854 accorded its support to the education of women, was greatly undermined by the national revolt of 1857. It was followed by an emphatic declaration of the policy of social and religious neutrality by Her Majesty the Queen, and Lord Stanley's Despatch of 1859 sounded a more cautious note. The official effort in support of the education of women was, therefore, slow to expand and not much could be achieved till 1870.

The indigenous efforts continued to work for popularizing female education. In 1860, the Parsi community of Bombay opened a number of Girls' Schools and worked for the cause with all sincerity and devotion. The various reform movements gave impetus to the spread of female education. The Brahmo Samaj had a good record of service in the field of education.

The prominent Brahmo members started publishing various journals with a view to promote education and culture among their women. The Arya Samaj made arrangements for women's education through institutions like Mahakanya Vidyalaya, Jullundher and many Arya Kanya schools in other parts of the country. The Prarthana Samaj and the Deccan Education Society made important contributions to the cause of female education. The Indian Social Conference, meeting every year with the annual session of the Indian National Congress, began to press the need for the extension of female education in the country and passed strong resolutions in its favour. The efforts of Pandita Ramabai, Maharshi Karve and Ramabai Ranade in the field of women's emancipation through education, were shedding their beams over the dark and mostly still waters of girls' illiteracy. Many other enlightened men and women began constructive programme for the spread of female education. They, in fact, devoted their time, energy and money for this pious cause.

The municipalities and the levy of the local fund cess gave impetus to the development of education for women. The inclusion of Indians in the Municipalities became helpful because, unlike the Britishers, they had no hesitation in spending money for the establishment and maintenance of Girls' Schools. Though the zeal of all the local bodies for the cause of women's education was not uniform, yet many of the local bodies did useful service to the cause of female education by establishing special Primary schools for girls. A great English social reformer, Mary Carpenter visited India and gave a new lead to the education of women. Her great contribution in this field was to suggest that training colleges for women teachers should be established, and that trained primary teachers should be employed in girls' schools in order to increase their potential and effectiveness. Her reputation as a social reformer and her direct access to the highest authorities, both in India and England, made it possible to give immediate effect to her proposals and the first Training College for women primary teachers came to be established by 1870. These colleges provided a condensed and intensive course of general education and formal pedagogic training and sent out their raw recruits as trained teachers after a period of 3 to 5 years. However, the encouragement which Mary Carpenter provided for the employment of women teachers gave inspiration to female education. It opened a very useful career for several women who were in need of remunerative jobs.

In spite of this progress, the gap between the education of men and women was still very wide. For boys at schools, the number of girls under instruction was 25 per cent only and that while one male adult out of 16 could read and write, only one woman in 434 could read and write. The Bethune School was extended to become a college. There were 81 secondary schools for girls in the country as a whole, of which only six were conducted by the Government. The total number of Primary schools was 2,600. The total enrolment of girls in special primary schools was 82,420. In Bombay, the number of female students were 21,859. In Madras they were 20,365 and in Bengal, the number were 17,452. Besides these, 42,071 girls were reading in co-educational primary schools. There were 15 training institutions for women primary teachers (with a total enrolment of 515 teachers) of which 4 were conducted by the Department of Education (two in Madras, two in Bombay).

Of these, Madras had 46 schools with 389 pupils; Bengal had 22 schools with 1,051 pupils; Bombay had 9 schools with 538 pupils; North-Western Province (U.P.) had 3 schools with 68 pupils; and Punjab had one school with 8 pupils.

Among aided schools three were in Madras, two in Bengal, three in North-Western Province and three in Punjab. It must also be noted that the principal burden of providing the necessary educational facilities to women depended heavily on private efforts because the Department only conducted 616 schools (with 24,291 pupils) out of a total of 2,697 institutions (with 1,27,066 pupils).

The Indian Education Commission discussed the problem of female education with great insight in 1881-82 and it pointed out that even in the most advanced States of India, 98 per cent of the female children of school-going age were still outside the schools, and that out the total female population covered by its enquiries, no less than 99.5 million were returned as unable to read and write. As such it therefore, stressed the need to give special treatment to the education of women and recommended the provision of larger funds for it from all sources—municipal, local or provincial. In order to attract more girls to schools and retain them for a longer period, it recommended liberal grant of concessions in fees, award of prizes, and institution of scholarships, especially for those who were above 12 years of age. As an encouragement to private effort, it recommended that conditions for the grant of aid to girls' schools should be easier, and the rates of grant in-aid higher than those prescribed for boys' schools. In order to encourage the employment of women teachers, a few points were suggested: (i) the adoption of pupil-teacher system, (ii) the establishment of additional normal schools under government control, (iii) the payment of liberal grants-in-aid to private schools and so on.

Training institutions were also conducted by private efforts and the offer was given to the wives of school masters to qualify themselves as teachers. The widows were trained as teachers for primary schools and the offer of liberal prizes were given to girls as well as to the teachers who trained themselves and would agree to become teachers. The grant of special assistance was given to girls' schools with hostels attached to it. Regarding the supervision of girls' schools, it was recommended that the organization and strengthening of a special Inspectorate was necessary to assess the work of girls as well as teachers. The inspectorate team were to be formed from among the educated women. It also recommended the adoption of special measures to promote the secondary education of girls.

The general opinion at this period was strongly in favour of differentiation of curricula for boys and girls and the Commission recommended (i) that the standards of instruction in girls' schools, whether primary or secondary, should be simpler than those for boys' schools; (ii) that they should be drawn up with special reference to the requirements of home life and the occupations open to women; and (iii) that special text looks should be prepared for girls schools.

The two decades following the Report of the Commission were a period of financial stringency, and it was not possible for the Government to organize special programmes for the development of education for women or to assign adequate grants for the purpose. The expansion of private enterprise was so great that, in spite of the lukewarm support from the government, the education of women evinced some progress by the end of the nineteenth century.

Even in 1901-02, the burden of providing educational facilities for girls lay heavily on private efforts. Of the 12 colleges for women, only one, the Bethune College, was conducted by the Government. Of the 422 secondary schools, as many as 356, were conducted by private efforts which also accounted for 3,982 girls' schools out of a total of 5,305.

A significant development of the nineteenth century was the opening of careers for women outside the home. The careers to be opened were that of teachers and nurses. A career in medicine was the next to be opened and in 1901-02 there were 76 women in medical colleges and 166 in medical schools. Besides, there were a fairly large number of women undergoing training of nurses, midwives, etc. An important event of this period was the creation of the Lady Dufferin Fund with the sole object of developing medical education among women. Liberal encouragement from other sources were also available at this time. Most of the students in medical and art courses were Europeans, Anglo-Indians, Indian-Christians and Zoroastrians. The Hindu and Muslim women had not yet taken to these careers. The education of women showed some progress during the next twenty years, mainly owing to the great public awakening created by the national struggle for independence and the First World War. The number of colleges increased in 1921-22 and the number of the students in medicine rose from 256 in 1902 to 905 in 1921-22.

Four colleges were established by the Government. Of the 675 Secondary schools—only 115 were conducted by the Government and more than 70 by the local bodies. Even at the Primary stage, the aided and unaided schools numbered 16,810 in the total of 21,956 institutions. The burden of providing education for women depended on private efforts. The extent of direct state effort had increased considerably between 1901 and 1921.

Another very significant development of this period was the considerable rise in the age of marriage, especially in the urban areas and among girls of the upper classes of society. This was due mainly to the pressure of changing social and economic circumstances and the progress of feminist movement in India. This trend was further increased by the demand of the educated men themselves to have educated wives, and preferably those who had been educated in secondary schools and colleges. M.E. Cousins writes: "The youngmen of the middle and upper classes insist on securing educated brides" Educated girls began to be preferred in marriage and the education of girls received a very strong impetus. Hindu and Muslim girls, therefore, began to attend the secondary schools and colleges in increasing numbers during this period.

The establishment of the Indian Women's University in Bombay by Maharshi D.K. Karve in 1916 with the help of a magnificent donation made by the late Sir Vithal Das Thackersey was an important milestone. It was originally an unrecognized private institution but it has since been raised to the status of a statutory University. It must be pointed out that women began to choose a number of new careers during this period. In 1901, their education was mostly restricted to the primary stage of learning and the main careers open to them outside the home were teaching and medicine. The careers in Science, Commerce and Agriculture, etc., were important additions during this period. The girls joined schools and colleges for training in technical and industrial careers. They also joined commercial and agricultural careers and entered the different respectable professions required by a civilized society.

A University Commission was appointed by Lord Curzon but it had nothing special to say about women's education. This was followed by the appointment of the Calcutta University Commission in 1916 popularly known as Sadler Commission. In 1919, the Commission made the first survey of women's higher education in Bengal and made recommendations for two distinct types of female education.

Scrutinizing the fifty years of the western system of

education and finding that it was merely a means for gaining Government jobs than to build character, the Indian leaders came forward with their own projects in the field of higher education. Banaras Hindu University was founded in 1911 with a women's wing attached to it. The Commission said that "The need of the vast majority who will spend their lives in Zenana, and their education will cease at an early age and who ought to be trained, on the one hand, to perform their Zenana duties with interest and knowledge, and on the other to understand and sympathize with the interest and work of their husbands, brothers; and secondly the need of the small but very important minority who will go out into the world to serve their fellows in professional calling or will play their part in the intellectual activities of the progressive section of Indian society and desire a high training to avail the opportunity different." Inspired by national feelings, the Muslims founded the famous Aligarh Muslim University. The Viswa Bharti was founded near Calcutta, Gurukul at Hardwar, and S.N.D.T. Women's University at Bombay. Many women began to appear in the examinations in different faculties of these universities.

The need for female education was widely acknowledged and the demand increased in volume. The women themselves realized that they should strive for a better standard life-style. In the words of the Maharani of Baroda, "Far and wide throughout the world today, a new energy is spreading amid the ranks of women of every class. Rich and poor, educated and ignorant, all alike feel the dawn of an era of fresh usefulness for their sex.... The women of the East, like the woman of the West may depend on this that in the proper use of education, lies the salvation of her sex. As long as she is ignorant, so long will she remain dejected, oppressed and incapable, if she organizes her efforts, she will respond to the changed environment."

Female education had to face three obstacles like apathy,

early marriage and lack of funds. The apathy was vigorously attacked by public propagation and the second was condemned by the passing of Sarda Act. Want of money which became a most formidable difficulty confronting the extension of women's education in British India was met by opening girls' schools financed by the Indians themselves and by popularizing co-education. Yet, in 1921, the disparity in literacy between men and women was persistently increasing.

Between 1922 and 1927, the increase in the number of girls under instruction was 400,000. It was a very substantial increase, but the increase in the number of male pupils was 24,00,000. Thus the difference between the number of boys and girls at school, already great, was increased by two million. Many girls attended boy's primary schools and some went to men's colleges. It was the most hopeful event and the Indians were happy to know about it.

The leading men and women came forward to declare aloud that the national prosperity and the place they desired India to occupy among the advanced nations of the world, depended on the women as well as the men of India becoming educated. All members, including the three Indians of the Hartog Committee (1928) went so far as to claim priority for girls' education.

The few educated women who had tasted the fruits of the new learning, sincerely felt that "education was a great social problem of India, and that until female education was lost under the restraints imposed upon it by Indian social traditions, India cannot attain the place to which she aspires as a modern nation." In the matter of women's education, therefore, the progress made during the last fifty years has been little short of marvellous. K. Natarajan writes, "It is a remarkable fact that while during and since the war, there has been, owing to the economic stress, some retardation of the advance in men's education, these causes have had little effect in checking the steady growth of the girls' education." Female education in India passed through total apathy, indifference, ridicule and criticism but finally it reached the point of ready acceptance. Rani Saheb of Sangli declared in 1927, "It may now be safely stated that anywhere in India, the need of education for girls as much as for boys is recognized as a cardinal need of progress—a sine-qua-non of national progress."

A changing trend towards female education became clearly visible due to the efforts and activities of All-India Women's Conference. The Maharani of Baroda in her presidential address underlined this transition when she noted that, "it is pleasing to watch the signs of the general awakening of interest throughout the country in the cause of the advancement of women.... In the field of education, especially higher education, there have been some brilliant achievements in individual area. Yet a few individual achievements, however, brilliant, cannot make up for the lack of general and well-ordered advancement of the women of the country in the matter of primary and secondary education."

There was a huge increase in demands for science subjects in higher studies which almost submerged the older domination of literary subjects. The vocational and technical subjects gained wide popularity. Referring to such changes Margaret Cousins remarks, "At least these are getting more demand due to the needs of the country, and to bring a fresh breeze into the stuffy atmosphere of girls' education of the past twenty years. They have also opened the door to the medical profession for those fortunate and brave enough to complete the difficult, costly and lengthy-degree courses."

The All-India Women's Conference largely became responsible for the reform in education for women. Its branches conducted adult women classes and the girls, schools. They also conducted classes for vocational training of women. In order to initiate reforms particularly in the curriculum of girls and to bring into existence a new type of college for Indian girls, the Lady Irwin Home Science College was founded in New Delhi to fulfill their aspirations.

The object was to enable women to utilize the advantages of science in their homes and to provide them the knowledge of Art interwoven with that particular heritage embodied in India's own culture and tradition, in its national games and dances, arts and crafts, sagas and songs and spiritual aspirations. The College took a firm hold on growing desires of parents for a curriculum for their girls, that is both— 'national' and groomed the young women to be new types of teachers, up-to-date home-makers and mothers, and capable organizers of public services, such as, their new status as responsible citizens.

The general interest in women's education led to the establishment of a number of schools and colleges exclusively for girls and the popularity of co-education even in the face of social restrictions existing in the country. M.E. Cousins insists that "the return to favour of co-education is a very hopeful sign of the times and promises to bridge the unnatural gulf that has existed between the sexes in India since the end of the Buddhist era." The growing recognition of the utility of education made the girls themselves eager for schools and colleges. Their mothers, having been denied education themselves, tried to secure it for their girls as a rule, specially in the urban areas.

The highest aim of women's education in India was considered to equip them to work freely and bravely with men; or if not with them then alongside them for the benefit of human race. In the very first Conference on Educational Reform, the women had themselves demanded that, "moral training based on spiritual ideals should be made compulsory for all schools and colleges." The general impression, though gaining ground in favour of female education, was that it did not favour women to become literary luminaries and scientific prodigies so as to enable them to question the superiority of men and claim equal rights with them. It was enough "if besides being loving and sweet spoken, they became helpful companions to their husbands in passing through the life's wilderness."

Education at the provincial level had been transferred to the control of Indian Ministers under the system of Diarchy. In 1937, Provincial autonomy was introduced. The States, then, began to take an increased interest in the promotion of education for women. Other favourable factors of the period that helped the spread of female education were the awakening among the people on account of the political struggle for Independence and the Second World War; a still further rise in the age of marriage, partly due to the Sarda Act but mainly due to social and economic pressures. The teachings of Mahatma Gandhi who dominated the history of those days and the phenomenal speed with which there spread the awakening in Indian women themselves. Prominent women founded a number of pioneering institutions for the overall progress in the field of female education.

However, in spite of all these favourable factors, the Government of India remained almost aloof and did not give any financial assistance to any project for educational development. The Indians primarily concentrated their efforts to emphasize on higher studies so as to open new opportunities of employment to the women.

Gradually, the trend towards co-education had increased very considerably. At the collegiate stage, more than 50 per cent of the total number of girls enrolled were studying in mixed institutions in 1946-47. The same may also be said of colleges for professional education. In the primary stage, the number of girls studying in mixed schools was even larger than the enrolment in separate institutions. In the secondary schools as well as in the special schools for technical, vocational and special education, the enrolment in separate institutions was much larger than those in mixed schools.

In 1947, the modern education of women was about a hundred and twenty five-years old. The evaluation of the achievements of this period can be done in two ways. The first is to compare the conditions that existed in India in 1800 to those that existed in 1946-47. This reveals a great achievement, both qualitative as well as quantitative. Educational opportunities were opened for women at all stages during this period. Their social status was raised to a considerable extent. Qualitatively, education had created among women a new self-awakening and awareness. It opened to them wider opportunities in life. But the progress of female education in India lagged behind the other progressive countries during the same period. The education of men was even backward if measured by the common standards in the West.

Another was the fact that a disproportionately large part of the advance in education of women was confined to the urban areas only. No school of any type had been set up in most of the Indian villages. The educational opportunities, as such, were denied, not only to women but to men as well. In many of the villages, only the mixed primary schools were in existence. Due to traditional prejudices, the rural girls were deprived of education.

It would be in the fitness of things to find out the reasons for the slow advance of education of women, and the wide gap that existed between it and the education of men, and for the comparative backwardness of rural areas. The decision of the Government to take no direct action in the matter and to leave the education of women mainly to the private efforts of the people adversely affected the pace of expansion. The people were pre-occupied with the freedom struggle of the country. Moreover, the expansion remained limited mostly to urban areas because hardly any private effort became available in rural areas. It generally remained still because no adequate machinery was created to deal with the important and stupendous task of female education. A significant advance in solving this problem would have been possible only if an adequate machinery had been created and if it had been helped by the Government on the one hand and the full co-operation of the people on the other.

The first of these was not possible under the over-cautious policy adopted by the British Government in regard to socio-religious matters of the people and the second was more or less ruled out by the political conditions of the day. Lastly, education, as a whole, starved for funds during the British period. The special problem like women's education, in fact, required very large funds which were never made available on some pretext or the other.

The awareness to obtain education and pursue careers, the women got an opportunity after 1947. Women became educated and trained for careers in various fields of life. There is hardly any field which has been denied to them. They have joined even the Army, Navy and the Air Force. Education has become, today, as the most important factor of a woman's empowerment. Women first joined as nurses, teachers, doctors and lawyers. At present they are serving big commercial concerns as CEO, and other significant high authorities. After completing MBA, they have opened their own business in jewellery, carpets and flowers. They have entered the 'space' while working in Space Research Institutes of India, USA and other countries. They are becoming self-reliant and extend financial support to their own families as well as they are serving the Nation. There is a plethora of women who have succeeded in competitive examinations. Thus, modern women enjoy complete equality in career-building at present.

Their entry to private entrepreneurship has increased by leaps and bounds. There appears a mushroom growth of colleges and universities run by men and women members of management committees. New courses like BBA, BCA, MBA, Medical, Para Medical and Engineering degrees have been started. The Computer Courses attract girls and boys both and they get new opportunities of employment as well as enjoying lot of perks and salary. Due to such an education which provides jobs, as well as satisfaction to large number of students have since then increased. These days the Indian boys and girls of well to do families are studying abroad for global recognition. The Indian students now go to USA, Germany, Britain and Australia for better training and education. These students include the girls too who fearlessly pursue their studies outside the country. After completing their education, they work in other countries with merit and efficiency.

9. Legal Enactments

In colonial India, the social status of women began to change gradually. Women were keen to stop their total dependence on men. The religious traditions had prescribed for them total humility and subordination to men in all matters. They were denied the opportunities of education and refinement as per the verdicts of the ancient law givers. Except a few women of the upper classes, the life of common women was not even worth living. The upper class women were also subjected to social evils like Sati, polygamy, etc. A rigorous life was expected of them, if they did not burn themselves alive with their dead husbands. In short, access to social justice and equality was not allowed to them.

The different Christian Missions saw the deplorable condition of women in the traditional society. They were amazed and emotionally moved to see their sad plight. With no share in property of the husband or their own father's, widows and the deserted women often earned their livelihood through joining the 'Kothas' in the cities. The Muslim women suffered a lot due to the easy system of 'divorce' in their community. They moved to their father's house after being divorced but various economic constraints of their family left them alone and helpless. They were too forced to join their unfortunate Hindu sisters on the 'Kothas'. With increase in the social evils among higher castes, the Indian society became quite orthodox and cruel towards women.

The Christian missions came to India to spread their religion. They opened schools, asylums, dispensaries and orphanages to give relief to the poor and the needy Indian people. They succeeded in converting mostly the lower classes of Indian people. They desired to save the widow from burning alive. They wanted to undertake a sort of "culturally motivated" device to end this crime. They informed about the pathetic scenes of the 'Sati' custom to the officers of the East India Company and pleaded to enact some laws to check the exploitation of Hindu women in the name of religion. The colonial administrators and writers produced enormous literature on Indian women's plight specially the inhuman custom of 'Sati'. They endeavoured to make surveys, and highlighted not only the barbarities but also the cruel custom of female infanticide. For a long time, the authorities of the East India Company refused to make any intervention in the socio-religious customs of the Hindus. In 1789, the colonial government set up an enquiry to investigate into the actualities of the practice of 'Sati'. As the Indian states had autonomous right to legislate for their subjects, the estate of Baroda was the first to enact a law against 'Sati' and 'Divorce'.

The State of Mysore passed a Bill to prevent infant marriages as early as 1894. It was the sincere desire of the native rulers to ameliorate the lot of Indian women. In 1933, the King of Mysore granted property rights to women in his own jurisdiction. He granted them the right of adoption. These bills were enacted in the states of Malabar and Travancore.

The Company's officers often brooded over the cruel social and religious 'sanctions' imposed upon the Indian women alone. Under the impact of western liberalism, they could not imagine that the inhuman customs practised in India possessed religious approval. To regenerate the Indian social system and to perform some 'good and civilized deeds', they encouraged the colonial masters to frame laws in order to save the women from atrocities. They questioned as to why morality and conjugal faithfulness are thrust upon women alone when the men were left free from any moral injunctions even for their similar lapses. The policy of one sided morality and the oppression and exploitation of women, led the Company's government to formulate some legislations for women. The educated and liberal Indians and their organizations fully supported the government in introducing the various reform bills. In the genesis of these reforms, as the colonial government claimed was "a civilizing motive." The colonial administrators attempted to recast the Indian patriarchy in order to make it convenient to women. They were enthusiastic towards their new mission. The Indian reformers invited their alien masters to work for social reforms. The women welcomed the legal measures not in any stress but because they thought that the reforms had roots in the Vedic equity of men and women.

Sati Abolition Act (1829)

The Supreme Court in Calcutta attempted to check the practice of 'Sati' within its jurisdiction. Realizing the horrors of Sati, the Danes at Serampur, the Dutch at Chinsura and the French at Chandranagore banned the practice of Sati in their jurisdiction. The officers of Bombay Presidency also banned this system in their regions. Some officers desired to approach the Governor General of India and genuinely requested him to intervene in the social system of the Hindus as they appeared quite irrational. They collectively wrote that "the human nature shudders at this crime" against Hindu women committed by their relatives and religious gurus. The Governor General realized the tragedy of 'Sati' but refrained from taking coercive methods to stop it. He advised the officers of the Company to work persuasively to stop it. In Bengal Presidency, the Magistrate of Midnapur wrote to the Governor in 1897 to enact a legislation to abolish this inhuman evil. He was also advised only to dissuade and convince the women to discard it. J.R. Elphinston again solicited the favour of the colonial government to issue a legal enactment to stop 'Sati'. Lord Wellesley received his letter and he decided to seek the views of the members of the Nizamat Adalat who were responsible for the detection and prevention of a crime within the British Presidencies. The members of the Nizamat Adalat consulted the learned Pandits who were well versed in Hindu jurisprudence. They opined that the widows of the three higher castes must burn themselves alive with their dead husbands. The Nizamat Adalat also suggested that a policy of 'abolition and compromise' would be a wise step on the part of the colonial Government. The Governor General issued circulars to prevent the custom of Sati in 1813, 1815 and 1917. The Police was directed to intervene and rescue the targets of Sati who were below 16 years in age or were pregnant.

Mr. Loushington, a magistrate in Madras presidency, wrote to the colonial Government in 1813 that a legal abolition of Sati would provide a "universal satisfaction" to all except a few conventional Purohits who earned a lot by presiding over the rituals of 'Sati'. Mr. Walter Ewer, another police officer of Lower India, sent an official letter to the Judicial Secretary in the colonial Government in 1818 and portrayed a very pathetic scene of Sati rites. He asserted that 'the widow without any friend to advise and protect her had no courage to protest against a crowd of hungry Brahmins.' In the end, he concluded that "such sacrifices have no spiritual bliss but a means of temporal joy of surviving relatives by enjoying the widow's share in property."

The members of Nizamat Adalat fully endorsed his views and they recommended immediate abolition of the custom of Sati specially in Dacca, Murshidabad, Bareilly, Allahabad,

Bundelkhand and Kalpi. At these places, the custom of Sati was not very common.

The Father of Indian Renaissance, Raja Rammohun Roy, had already taken up the issue of Sati and he consistently made efforts to convince the Hindus that the custom had no sanction of religion. He extensively wrote about its non-Shastric origin and through his two newspapers, 'Sambad Kaumudi' and 'Bangdoot', he created a lot of public opinion against Sati in the face of mighty opposition from the people of Bengal under the orthodox leadership of Raja Radha Kant Deb. In 1822, Rammohun Roy widely circulated his "Brief Remarks Regarding Modern encroachments on the Ancient Rights of Females According to Hindu Law of Inheritance." The then Governor General wrote in 1827, "Sati could be abolished only by an improvement of people in India, and diffusion of knowledge among the Indians." In July, 1828, Lord William Bentinck became the Governor General of India. He was 'a reformer by temperament' and he became indeed more serious on the issue of Sati than his predecessors.

William Bentinck consulted different sections of Indian people, his officers in army and the judiciary, as well as the members of his Executive Council. He also consulted Raja Rammohun Roy, who left this problem upon Bentinck's shoulders and its suitability for the colonial Government. The Governor General was quite convinced of the necessity of a legislation to stop this crime. Later the Governor General in Council finally concluded that, "We are decidedly in favour of an open, avowed and general prohibition of Sati resting altogether upon the goodness of the Act and our power to enforce it." On 4th December 1829, by the Regulation XVI of the colonial Government, the custom of Sati was totally abolished. The Sati Abolition Act was thus legislated in 1829. Similar enactments were passed in Madras and Bengal Presidencies.

Bentinck sought the help of Raja Rammohun Roy and asked him to publicise the good points of the new Act. Raja

Rammohun popularized the Act of 1829 through his writings and speeches, and created a mighty public opinion in its favour. He removed the misconceptions of the people about the Act of 1829. Raja Radhakant Deb gathered the support of some orthodox men like Nilmony De, Gokulnath Mallick, Ramgopal Mallick and Bhabani Charan. They went to meet the Governor in a delegation. They sent petitions to the Governor General in Council and to the King in Council. About 120 Pandits and Purohits along with 346 men from places near Calcutta sent a petition for the immediate withdrawal of the Act. When a delegation of the orthodox leaders waited upon the Governor General, Lord Bentinck asked for a piece of paper and he wrote on it—"WIDOWS ARE NOT COMMANDED BY HINDU RELIGIOUS SCRIPTURES TO DESTROY THEMSELVES". He did not meet the delegation headed by Radhakant Deb. He immediately sent the piece of paper on which he had written these words to the members of the delegation. The appeal of the orthodox men was totally rejected even in the Privy Council. The Raja celebrated the victory of women at Jorasanko in a meeting of Brahmos. He also sent letters of thanks to the Privy Council and to William Bentinck the same day. The impact of the Sati Abolition Act was so great that the Nizam of Hyderabad banned Sati in his territories in 1858. Bentinck's role was really commendable. He took a great risk, but he became successful in his task.

The Raja of Satara abolished Sati in his State and Lord Dalhousie offered his support to the legislations against Sati. He pressurized the Rajput rulers of Alwar, Doongarpur, Bikaner and Udaipur to enact legislations to ban Sati immediately. The Sati Abolition Act worked from 1930 onwards with enormous contentment among the Indians. The practice of Sati disappeared from India but stray cases are often reported even now.

Widow Remarriage Act (1856)

The deplorable condition of upper caste Hindu widows forced them to hold that death was a preferable choice for them because it made them once for all free from all sorrow, sin and suffering of life. It was a tradition in India that lower caste widows could re-marry the brother or father of the deceased husband. The patriarchal society took it for granted that the widows had voracious sexual appetite. They wanted to get rid of the widows and this had made Sati a compulsory rite. The evil of infanticide was also curbed and the misconceptions regarding it were removed. In 1830, the Law Commission under the Chairmanship of Macaulay concluded that the prohibition of remarriage and the high rate of female infanticide are inter-related. Infanticide was later taken to be a separate problem for separate reasons as attention was given specially to the issues of marriage, dowry, rape and kidnapping etc. of the young girls.

It was generally believed that remarriage of a widow was a sin according to Hindu Shastras as "it involved guilt and disgrace on earth and exclusion from heaven." The Law Commission, in the beginning, had forwarded the sentiments of the orthodox Pandits. An eminent reformer, Ishwar Chandra Vidya Sagar mobilized the public opinion in favour of widow remarriage and sent several appeals to the Colonial Government for Hindu marriage reforms, including the abolition of Kulinism and polygamy. Quoting from various Hindu Shastras, he wrote a book entitled 'Marriage of Hindu Widows' which was declared by the orthodox section of Hindus as highly prejudicial. Many other influential Hindus like Raja Raj Ballabh of Dacca attempted to introduce remarriage for widows. The efforts of the Indian reformers were cursed by the orthodox men of Hindu society. They not only opposed but violently criticized these efforts. The reformers tried their best to prove that the custom of remarriage was approved by Hindu Law. Quoting from the Shastras, Vidya Sagar attempted to prove that the practice of remarriage existed in ancient India and he is not propagating any innovation. It has been creditable that Vidya Sagar could win the majority of the people to his side. A well drafted petition was sent by him in this regard to the Colonial Government. The British responded well and the Hindu Remarriage Act was enacted in 1856. Many widows became its beneficiaries. For the first time the widows specially those who belonged to the high caste families felt some relief. Pandita Ramabai wrote a book, *The High Caste Hindu Widow* which received wide circulation and it created a sound public opinion in favour of Widow Remarriage. Yet, it is a fact that the number of such marriages were not very high in the country The widows themselves realized that work opportunities and education were far more beneficial to them than their remarriage. The efforts of Malabari, Phule, Karve and some other reformers deserve special mention in making the Indian widows to realize the fact that education and employment in various professions like Teachers, Nurses, Doctors and Advocates were indeed an honourable course for their safe future. Swami Dayanand also recommended the education and rehabilitation of the Hindu widows. The high caste widows had become wise enough and they wished to acquire the control and management of their landed property which would offer them economic independence as well as social respect. They were saved from going back to the inferior position in the domestic fold. As long as the widows did not marry, the landed property and other facilities were provided to her from the husband's side. They were retained in the houses of their in-laws, perhaps to maintain and confirm their chastity. It was required to make them an 'honest' widow. They often lost property due to the conspiracy and manoeuvrings of their relatives specially when they remarried outside the husband's family.

Pandita Ramabai mentioned about Rakmabai's case in the Bombay High Court that "the learned and civilized judges are determined to enforce, in this enlightened time, the inhuman laws enacted in the barbaric time, since four thousand years ago.... There is no hope for women in India whether they live under Hindu rule or British rule." She added, "we can not blame the British Government for not defending a helpless woman. The reforms they are introducing are in agreement with the male population of India."

Rakmabai wanted separation from her aged and idle husband but she lost the case and her husband got restitution of conjugal rights from the Court. The men collected a large sum of money to help her husband named Dadaji Bhikaji. Rakma preferred going to jail than to go with her husband. Her husband won the case under the newly enacted Act XV of 1877. Ramabai widely circulated the helplessness of widows even under a colonial rule which highly claimed for itself to be the 'Saviour' of the suffering Hindu women.

Ban on Female Infanticide (1795 and 1870)

During the period of colonial Rule in India, Rajasthan, Punjab, U.P., Bihar and Bengal were widely under the sway of the evil of female infanticide. It has been mainly a Rajput custom but even the Muslims (Saiyyads) practised it. It mostly persisted in the lower middle classes of Indian society. The Khatris, Bedis, Sodhis and Jats also practised this evil. It is wrong to say that in Government reports based on the survey of 'different cities and rural regions', the cases of Infanticide have been exaggerated by the British. It is an open fact that this crime is still prevalent through the system of modern medical technology. The first step of the Colonial Government was to obtain undertakings from the Rajas and chiefs of different states to check and abolish this custom. In the name of their security, the little girls were harshly killed. Dowry was also a major cause of the murder of a female child. The son was welcome for he was authorized to perform the last rites of the parents, according to Hindu Shastras.

William Carey, who himself saw the horrors of infanticide in Calcutta, submitted a report to Governor Wellesley after the survey of different areas. It was the Government of Bombay who first legislated the Regulation No. XXI to ban the crime of infanticide. Two other Regulations (in 1802 and in 1804), were issued which banned infanticide and declared it a crime. Those who indulged in it were to be treated as criminals and punished. The colonial administrators appointed special Chowkidars and provided them with adequate staff and necessary amenities like lanterns and lathis. They also appointed an officer in every village to maintain Registers of births and deaths. The British followed the persuasive as well as coercive methods to save the girl child from being killed just after her birth.

The colonial Government passed the special Act to abolish infanticide in 1870. Due to its stringent provisions, it proved very effective in curbing this crime in North West Provinces and Rajputana. The native Rajas cooperated with the colonial administrators in their efforts. This Act is also known as Strachey's Bill. The confidence with which the colonial government's effort entered the most private chamber of women's apartments in the Hindu families deserves admiration. The government's efforts yielded effective results. The British officers adopted educative programmes and also restricted the marriage expenditures. The census of 1888 reported that the practice of female infanticide had almost stopped (It has reincarnated in modern times with new technological inventions killing the girl child in the womb itself).

Native Marriage Act III (1872) and Age of Consent Bill (1891)

In 1829, the Colonial administrators declared rape as an offence under the Indian Penal Code. The punishment for this crime was death. In 1846 rape was redefined to cover the husbands who consummated marriage with an under-age wife. Many reformers like Vidya Sagar and Keshub Chandra Sen condemned the custom of child marriage in their speeches and writings. According to the reformers, the institution of child marriage was based on "outmoded Shastras." In 1850, the colonial administrators fixed the age of the girls at 10 for the consummation of marriage and before 10 as "rape" and made it punishable under Article 376 of IPC. The educated Indians and many reform Associations began fresh debates on 'Women and tradition'. Maharaja of Burdwan sent a petition to the colonial government and another to the Legislative Council to abolish polygamy practised in Indian families. Many Hindus too wanted marriage reforms and demanded legislation in this regard. In 1872, the colonial Government enacted the Native Marriage Act III which fixed the age of Marriage for girls at 14 and for boys at 18. It also contained provisions to ban 'polygamy'. Some of its clauses provided for legal allowance to women after they were divorced. The Act indirectly encouraged inter-caste marriages but a reference to the caste was ignored. The progressive section of Indian intelligentsia welcomed the useful provisions of this Act.

The age of consent was widely debated for many years in India under the British rule. Opinions were polarized on the issue of consummation of marriage even when education spread, specially, among the Indian men. Behramji Malabari, Veeresalingam Pantulu, M.G. Ranade, Gidumal and many other reformers extensively wrote and attempted to mould the public opinion in favour of raising the 'Age of consent'.

Malabari wrote notes on infant marriages and Enforced Widowhood in 1884. In 1891, the Indian Penal Code and Criminal Procedure Code covered this reform under its purview and issued instructions under different sections. It is notable that fifty nine women doctors sent an appeal to the Viceroy of India to fix the age of consent at 14 for girls on medical grounds. Apart from them, more than two thousand Indian women sent a forceful petition to Queen Victoria to stop child marriages through some legal enactment. The British passed the Age of Consent Bill in 1891 which was further amended in 1925. It was an irony that an alien government framed legislations to eradicate this evil, though it would have been better if Indians themselves could take reformative positive steps in this field specially on grounds of health.

Married Women's Property Act III (1874)

This Act, legislated by the British, was quite revolutionary in the sense that it provided for the Indian females the right to possess and manage their own 'landed property' and estates and to be the guardians of their children. The women were authorized by this Act, to acquire and manage their own property. They could inherit landed property from their father as well as from their mother's side. The clauses of this Act encouraged the women to join remunerative work and enter respectable professions. They were allowed to join the legal and medical professions after qualifying the examinations. They could purchase and sell their landed property. It was for the first time that the Indian women could acquire property in their own names. The Act of 1874 declared that the wages and earnings of a married woman were exclusively her own. No male member could snatch away her income. Women were granted, by this Act, the recognition as Managers and Proprietors of their landed property. They issued orders to the 'Munshi' and paid taxes in their own name. The women Tallukadars worked with merit and talked even to the British officers about their problems and difficulties. The Act created a favourable environment for the women to practise respectable vocations and adopt a useful work-culture to lead a decent, dignified and respectable life. It gave them an opportunity to unfold their best talents and to keep their raiyyats satisfied. They established themselves as "socially useful and nationally needed individuals."

Abolition of Devdasi System (1929)

The Central Legislature of India enacted this law in 1929 to end the degenerated system of Devdasis. The state of Travancore abolished the practice of Temple dancing in 1930. The Bombay Legislature also passed a legal enactment to stop the immoral practice of prostitution. Efforts were made to rehabilitate these women in a new and respected life-style. The age-long exploitation of women by mahants and purohits was publicly challenged and efforts were made to stop it.

Restriction on Immoral Traffic of Women (1937)

The Legislature of Bengal was the first to enact this legislation. In accordance with the Act, Protective Homes were established where the rescued women could lead a decent life with dignity. They were often married (if they wished so) to suitable men. Such Acts were passed in Madras and Punjab in 1935 and Mysore in 1936.

Hindu Law of Inheritance Act (1929 and 1937)

The Travancore Succession Act was passed in 1916, and the Cochin Succession Act was passed in 1927. In 1929, an amendment was made in the property rights which gave the women to function under the protection of their family and the government both. Yet, they could have the inherited property under their own name and care. The Act was again amended in 1937. Under both the laws, the scope of property was enlarged for them. In case of separate property, the Hindu widow was given the same share as received by the son. In order to keep the ownership of the land in the same family, the widows were permitted to marry within the same family to which her husband belonged. The government of Punjab thus desired to check the fragmentation of land in their own economic interest. The reformers said that the amendment was introduced to safeguard the patrilineal hold over the property. Under this system, the custom of polyandry and the custom of the father marrying the widow of his own son or brother marrying the widowed sister-in-law became common.

The widow was granted maintenance if she stayed in the household of her deceased husband where, they thought, her chastity was ensured. The Act reduced the possibilities of illegal relationship outside marriage and it also checked the evil of infanticide.

The law, though, was intended to make an "honest widow" but it often resulted in making them a "propertyless widows." An article 'Stree Purush Tulna' written by Tara Bai and 'the High Caste Hindu Widow' written by Pandita Ramabai throw light on the dissatisfaction of women on the amendment of this Act. A voice of revolt was raised against the system which forced the women alone to shoulder the burden of perfection and morality. The British Government, to safeguard its imperialistic motives, sided with the Indian males. The colonial masters were ready to interfere in the system of patriarchal ideologies prevalent in India only to uphold their own self-interest.

Law of Adoption Act (1935)

The Bombay Legislature enacted this law and granted the

Indian women, the right of adoption. It was a right given in ancient times to the couple who did not have children.

Sanction of Birth Control Clinics (1935)

These clinics of special types were functioning in big cities and the government granted them necessary legal sanction to function in the interest of women's health and welfare.

Hindu Divorce Bill (1928)

On demand of various women's organizations like All India Women's Conference, the law on Divorce was legalized. Earlier the women who were troubled by their husbands and relatives had no divorce right. The British government enacted the Hindu Marriage Dissolution Bill to save the women from the exploitation by their husbands.

Factory Acts

The transformation of the economy of India under the British rule affected the life of Indian women who joined the industries as labourers and worked in various factories and mines. Not only did they work in the fields of cash crops and other agricultural sector but they also worked in various factories and mills. They formed about 25 per cent of the total labour in India. As such, the British government, on demand of various women organizations, passed a number of legal enactments to improve their service conditions, salary and welfare including the period of work.

Regulation and Inspection of Mines Act VIII (1901)

This Act ensured the safety of women labour. The Indian Mines Act of 1901, 1923 and 1928 regulated their hours of work. Their labour in underground mines was banned in 1929. (It was reimposed in 1947.)

Factory Act (1911)

The working condition of women labour in cotton and jute mills were regulated by the Indian Factories Act of 1911. It banned their work in the night shifts. This Act was amended in 1923 and in 1928 by which the period of their duty were reduced to 8 hours only.

Factory Act of 1934

It gave some concessions to women of the labour sectors. It provided them with maternity leave and other benefits related with it. In Madras, the Maternity Benefit Act was enacted in 1935 when the women labour were given some extra money during the period of maternity and delivery under maternity benefits scheme.

It is a fact that the road to the mansion of social justice and equality was full of disagreements, dissensions, disparities, distress and dangers for the Indian women. The reformers as well as the women activists themselves realized that mere legal enactments were not enough. Education and awareness were required and not just the legal enactments. The graph of female education increased to some extent but the percentage in female education did not keep pace with the desired goal and therefore the reforms and legal enactments remained mere 'scrap on paper'.

We may conclude that:

(a) The Christian Missions worked hard to save the women from the rigorous social customs said to be observed under the Shastrik injunctions. In the form of legal enactments, the British Officers provided them 'some liberal space' to stand with honour and get rid of Sati, Infanticide and unequal marriages etc.

(b) The British could not level up the gender discrimination in India. Yet in colonial India, the women's world was surely enlarged. The women, specially belonging to the urban middle classes could receive education and develop a positive approach to life. They could join different vocations to be self-dependent and courageous.

(c) Under the colonial rule the women began their journey towards economic and social transformation. They became quite inspired to participate in the freedom struggle of India. Their courage and bravery were admired in the world. It was Gandhiji who invited and encouraged their participation in the Indian national movement so much so that they even forgot about their own women's movement. They fought bravely for the freedom of their country.

(d) The colonial administrators took initiative in putting the problems of women to the forefront of the then socio-political scenario. Since then, women's issues became as pertinent and crucial as national questions of the day.

(e) The British rulers enacted some legislations which were not only related to women's uplift but they also opened vistas of opportunity for them. A list of some other legislations is mentioned below:—

(i) The Guardians and Wards Act (1860)
(ii) Indian Penal Code (1860)
(iii) Christian Marriage Act (1872)
(iv) Indian Evidence Act (1872)
(v) The Workmen Compensation Act (1923)
(vi) The Women's Practitioners Act (1923)
(vii) The Indian Succession Act (1923)
(viii) The Payment of Wages Act (1936)

(ix) The Muslim Personal Law (Shariat) Application Act (1937)

After the attainment of independence in 1947, India accepted the system of Parliamentary Democracy and adopted a Constitution in 1950. The new Constitution granted to the Indian women total equality in matters of civil, political and economic rights. Yet, the status and position of women in India remained more or less the same. Inspite of the reforms enunciated in colonial India and the courage and bravery of women in the freedom struggle, the equality granted to them by the Constitution, could not take a concrete shape. The reformers from Rammohun Roy to Gandhi could not change their total lot and their social equality remained only a dream. Their own efforts, through their own organizations like AIWC could not bring satisfactory change. Their wish to organize a women's movement in India remained only a half fulfilled task. Their agenda again attracted the attention of the Indian Parliament and many programmes of women's welfare were adopted. Ameliorative measures were adopted for the women in the Five Year Plans of the country and the Government of India attempted to improve their conditions. The National Social Board was constituted to look after the women's welfare. A network of social welfare departments was established in almost all the states of India for women's health care, security and childrens' care etc.

In free India, many Acts related to women's welfare were amended. Amongst such legal enactments, the Special Marriage Act was amended in 1954. The Factories Act was amended in 1948 and the Employees' State Insurance Act and the Minimum Wages Act was amended in 1948. Some very useful legislations enacted for them in free India are as under:

(a) Hindu Marriage Act (1961)
(b) Hindu Succession Act (1961)

(c) Hindu Minority and Guardianship Act (1961)
(d) Hindu Adoption and Maintenance Act (1961)

A few other Acts related to women's cause are as under:—

(a) The Plantation Labour Act (1951)
(b) The Cinematograph Act (1951)
(c) Special Marriage Act (1954) and Hindu Marriage Act (1955)
(d) The Maternity Benefit Act was enacted in 1961 and amended in 1995
(e) Beedi and Cigar Workers' Condition of Employment Act (1966)
(f) The Foreign Marriage Act (1969)
(g) The Indian Divorce Act (1969)
(h) The Medical Termination of Pregnancy Act (1971)

It is notable that in the Code of Criminal Procedure changes have been introduced for the social security of women. Some legal enactments that were concerned only with the labour women are as under:

(a) The Bonded Labour Abolition Act (1976)
(b) The Contract Labour Act (1979)
(c) Equal Remuneration for Equal Work (1976)
(d) Employment Conditions Act (1979)

The legal enactments, related to the welfare of their children are as under:

(a) The Infant-milk Substitutes Act (1992)
(b) The Child Labour Act (1986)
(c) Juvenile Justice Act (1986)

The Child Marriage Restraint Act, enacted in the Colonial India, was amended in 1978 and the age of marriage for girls was raised from 15 to 18 and for boys it was raised from 18 to 21. To break its implementation was declared a cognizable offence. The Maternity benefit scheme was amended in 1976 when more benefits were provided to women, during the maternity period. 'The Factories Amendment Act of 1976 provided the compulsory arrangement for creches where 30 women were employed in a factory. This act was applicable to the mine workers too. The Work and Wages Act of 1958 was initiated by the Central Social Welfare Board by which NGOs were provided with financial assistance to take up a wide variety of income generating activities by women in groups. In 1975, the concepts of vocational training were added to this programme which aimed at the training and skill development of the poor class women and provided them with the opportunities to be the Teachers, Bal Sevikas, Workers of Anganbari and Nurses etc. Many schemes were introduced for women in the age group of 18 to 30. 'Asha facility' has been introduced for pregnant women.

Rehabilitation Centres (1977)

For destitute women Rehabilitation Centres were established in 1977. Women in the age of 18 to 50 were provided with the facilities to live and learn different crafts to enter a respectable vocation and lead a financially independent life.

Integrated Child Development Service (1979)

A National Children's Fund was established for conducting special Nutritional Programmes. Day care services are provided to the children of working class and ailing mothers. All these projects are working on an All India level since 1985.

Hostels for Working Women (1976)

Hostels have been built for the working women. The objective of these attempts have been to provide a secure living place to the lonely women.

Employment and Income Generating Units (1982)

For war widows and for women living below poverty line, many income generating projects have been sanctioned by the Central Social Welfare Board. This reform has already been implemented.

Voluntary Action Bureau (1984)

These have been set up throughout the country to combat the atrocities done to women. It also provides preventive and rehabilitative measures to the victims.

Legal Enactment against Rape and Exploitation (1983)

A number of Amendment Bills were passed by the Indian Parliament in 1983 by which the clauses of Indian Penal Code and Criminal Procedure Code were made more stringent and effective against the crime of rape and cruelty against women.

The National Commission for Women has been established in 1990. There were two core units in it which worked to safeguard the rights of women. Complaints Cell deals with dowry, dowry-death, torture, desertion, bigamy, rape, refusal to register FIR, incest, cruelty of male family members, discrimination in employment and domestic violence. Its working has not been very satisfactory.

Since 1993, the organization conducts, through NGOs, the system of Family Courts better known as 'Parivarik Mahila Lok Adalat'. Legal awareness programmes are also launched from time to time for Police, NGOs and concerned officers. It organizes sensitizing programmes for all of them. It looks after the release and rehabilitation of women prisoners. Rehabilitation of widows as well as of prostitutes and their children have been the objective of the Commission. It also works for women's participation in electoral process and custodial justice for women prisoners. Basically, it deals with issues of violence on women. It works for the anti-dowry move and lays emphasis upon employment of women in agriculture and in other technological institutions. The Commission also assures the rights of the women of minority classes.

In fact, many of the legal enactments and the plans and programmes for women's uplift gained speed after the UN declared 1975 as International Women's year. The year 1975 was observed with enthusiasm throughout the world. A Women's Decade followed and every year, 8th of March is observed as International Women's Day. The Indian government came up with a National Perspective Plan for women in 1988. The health, education, political participation and social upliftment of women have been taken as important units in it.

Panchayati Raj Bill (1989)

Indian women conducted the Suffrage Movement from 1917 onwards and they got right to vote and stand for election in 1921. Madras Legislature was the first to provide women with political rights. All other States also granted political rights to women. In 1989, the Government granted 30% Reservation for Women in Panchayats in the rural regions and Nagar Nigams. The rural women have been involved in the decision-making process and they have felt real empowerment. They are elected 'Pradhans' in the villages. They adopt programmes of women's welfare through the Panchayats. In 1990, they adopted the Dwacra Scheme for the part time employment and development of rural women. The scheme provides them with economic empowerment.

The Mahila Kosh

It has been an innovative plan to enable the rural females to learn various skills and earn honest money through it. In 1990, the Indian women were provided the full co-operation of the government for improvement of health and education. Besides maternity benefits and child care, they are provided knowledge in nutrition and population education which gives them an opportunity to increase their experience and improve their mental plane.

The Department of Family Planning was established in 1966. Under IVth and Vth Plan periods, programmes of child care, mass-education, motivation services and supplies, training workers, research and evaluation were conducted by this Department. NGOs associated themselves with different work under the Government care.

The Indian government ratified the UN Convention of Elimination of all forms of Discrimination against women in 1993. The Indian Government endorsed the Mexico Plan for Action in 1975 and the Nairobi Forward Looking strategies in 1985. The Beijing Declaration and Platform for Action was adopted by the Indian Government in 1995. India has also signed the Gender Equality and Development for Peace Programme in 1995.

The Indian Ministry of Human Resource Development assigned a separate section for women. There is now a separate department of Women and Children working under it as Ministry of Women and Child Development. Women study centres have been established in Universities and Colleges with regular financial aid from the Ministry. It launched the 'Balika Samriddhi Yojana' in 1997. The Government of India launched the Women Development Cells and Cooperative Banks for them in 1995.

For the empowerment of women, the Government of India adopted a major strategy for women's development in the 10th Five Year Plan. It is a concentrated plan and some of its strategies are as under:

For Social Empowerment:

1. Health and Family Welfare.
2. Education and Training.
3. Welfare and Development.
4. Women and Media.
5. Women and Environment.
6. Women's participation in Science and Technology.
7. Awareness of gender sensitization.

For Economic Empowerment:

1. Women in Agriculture and Management.
2. Poverty Removing Programmes for Poor Women.
3. Employment and Income Generation.
4. Women in Small Scale and Cottage Industry.
5. Help to women in Unorganized and Informal Sectors.
6. Increase in the participation of women in all services.
7. Micro Credit Scheme for Women.

For Gender Justice:

1. Eradication of Sex-related harmful practices.
2. Access to Health, Education and Employment.
3. Access and Control on productive measures.
4. To make women's merit visible.
5. Adoption of Gender Budgeting.
6. Effective enforcement of various legislations in favour of Women.
7. Increased number of women in the process of decision making.
8. To check all sorts of violence against women.

Indian women attained their political right in the Central and Provincial Legislatures by the Act of 1935. At present they possess equal rights with men to fight elections for Indian Parliament and State Legislatures. They are appointed as members of foreign delegations. They act as Governors and

Vice-Chancellors. They are also nominated to Rajya Sabha and Legislative Councils. The Panchayat elections brought over 7,00,000 women with full political empower-ment. 3,00,000 women representatives reached Nagar Nigams and Municipal Boards through the Panchayati Raj Act. How thrilling it is to note that Mrs. Pratibha Patil has been elected Hon'ble President of India in 2007 and Ms. Miera Kumar has been elevated as the speaker of Lok Sabha.

The National policy for Empowerment of women came in 2001. It inspired the Indian women to attain perfection and merit to lead the future world. For their empowerment, education and refinement are ample opportunities. The women's movement and a wide network of the NGOs having vision and insight are contributing to the task of women's empowerment. Yet, one can say with a heavy heart that there exists an enormous gap between the goals enumerated in the Constitution, the legal enactments, attractive policies for them and the real situational position of Indian women today. Some women reaching the heights cannot be the criteria of the changed socio-economic position of all women. Betterment through legal enactments are only passed on paper by the Government. In 2002, women's representation in Rajya Sabha has been as low as 7.5% to 11.5%. Women's representation in state legislatures is less than 5% in many states. The crime graph against women is on the increase. It has forced the Indian Government to enact the Domestic Violence Bill in 2006. Almost all legal enactments have loopholes and there are instances of women's ignorance as they do not know about these enactments. The scenario becomes all the more disappointing when we all read in the newspapers the cases of rape and incest. It is true that the women are themselves responsible for some of their problems. They do not wish to come out of the shell that has grasped them from all sides. They possess greed and temptation to lead a luxurious life even at the cost of their mental and moral agony. The women in general except some, have not shown any sincere urge to develop and so all legal enactments for their development appear quite useless. The census of 2001 reveals that the rate of female education has been only 54.16%. All plans, programmes and legal provisions for women are futile if they do not know and they do not wish to use them perhaps for maintaining a false traditional face in society.

The question arises, what to do? Everyone must try to resolve this question. For sexual harassment at work place a Prevention Act was enacted in 2000, according to which a Complaint Committee was to be constituted and it was to be headed by a woman and half the members of the committee were to be women. Almost all institutions have yet to implement this. Even today there is a conspiracy to insist and maintain the chequered patriarchal setup of Indian family about which Pandita Ramabai frankly and aptly complained as back as 1880 in the Bombay High Court.

'The truth remains that we must keep our houses and society in perfect order. No foreigner should get any opportunity to come and sarcastically interfere in our social system and humiliate the inmates of a country which has long been known for spiritual and human values. Let us be awakened and aware to the temporal and scientific knowledge about our ownselves and let us keep pace with the progress of human values along with the progress in the fields of Science and Technology which may open vistas of new knowledge to all of us. It is inevitable to maintain the values of Indian culture which provide us the very roots of our own existence and life.'

10. The Excellence

After a long struggle, pain and hard labour, the women in this country excelled in the mission of representing the modern awakening through excellence in different fields. The Indian women secured equality of status with men as embodied in the Constitution of free India. The real advance was marked by the change in men's outlook towards them and their own role in the socio-political set-up of the country. The women's movement in India, definitely heralded a glorious era when it vividly revealed the great qualities of Indian womanhood, hitherto lying dormant. There grew a broad social consciousness among the Indian women and they felt an inner call and urge to serve the Motherland. They ultimately realized that their mission in life did not end only with becoming good wives or mothers. They gladly accepted their new position as useful members of the body politic of a civilized community. Thousands of women came out to actively undertake various responsible jobs outside their homes and proved their worth and merit.

They prepared themselves to discharge the sublime duties of an awakened womanhood of a great country. The women's new role in India, therefore, rightly struck a new path and heralded a new vision. It aroused in the hearts of women, new hopes and aspirations of service in the wider arena of global life. They then, began to work effectively for bringing peace and prosperity for the entire globe. The new ideals, in fact, enabled them to attain the ultimate goal of self-realization and of rare excellence.

The suffering women of India received the first relief when ideas and achievements of the West began to penetrate deep into the country. The liberal humanitarianism of the West provided a healing balm to the bleeding sores of the Indian women. The rational spirit and scientific enquiry led to a fresh analysis of their weal and woe. The Western impact, on the one hand brought about a correct diagnosis of the long-existing ills and on the other it provided a real remedy to them. The West, no doubt, unfolded the secrets of India's glory and greatness, when it began to be commonly upheld that during the Rig Vedic age the women enjoyed equal status with men and they were considered as the useful members of society. During the period of the greatest degradation of Indian womanhood, the West, succeeded in creating a deep stirring of conscience among the Indian intelligentsia.

When the inherent values of Indian culture were revived under impetus from the West, the socio-religious and political thinkers of the country began to adopt a liberal attitude towards women. They came forward to initiate the much-needed useful social reforms to safeguard the status and position of Indian women. These reforms were introduced by them with the firm belief that India's progress was closely linked with women's advancement. They declared openly that if India has to develop it must be accompanied with awakened and developed women of India. They declared openly that if India wished to recapture the greatness of the 'past', women should be allowed to fully share the burden of the arduous tasks. As such, the recognition of the right of women to complete equality opened up new avenues of progress which encouraged women to play an increasingly effective role in all walks of the country's life.

The new ideas of progress and self-consciousness dawned upon the women's horizon, and women's strong desire for 'change' became discernible. At first, it reflected itself in the pioneering efforts of individual women leaders like Pandita Ramabai and Ramabai Ranade. Later it was represented through various women's organisations which united them together for their cause. The outstanding among these organizations was the All India Women's Conference which took up the cudgels against irrational orthodoxy, injustice, and discrimination and it worked most successfully in the field of women's education and career. The renowned Irish women Mrs. Margaret Cousins and Annie Besant were equipped with experience and practical wisdom who came to fan the flames of the Indian feminist movement. By their contribution towards educational expansion and political freedom and by their championship of the cause of women in general, both of them won a lasting place in the gender history of India.

When the enthusiasm for political freedom gained momentum, it was fully realized that freedom for women was an integral part of the freedom for the nation. The women of India had emerged successful in both these objectives. In the Suffrage Movement they succeeded only because the Indian men were liberal enough to recognize the worth of the cooperation of their better halves. The women had thrown themselves whole-heartedly into the fight for political independence of the country. They had shown their finer capabilities and their strength to suffer patiently and boldly the tortures and privations of life. Their participation in politics paved the way for their complete emancipation and freedom from traditional bondages. With increased opportunities of education, the Indian women developed the highest and best of their latent qualities and emerged on the changing scenario to spread the sweet fragrance of betterment in all spheres of national life.

The impact of education on the economic status of women proved as strong as its impact on other social aspects of their life. Women's economic horizon, once limited to household chores and labour, expanded considerably as she joined various vocations after completing education and training.

Women's first response after receiving education was to the call for teachers and nurses. The opportunities for women to become teachers owe a great debt to the work of Christian missions as well as to purely Indian movements for training women, such as conducted by the Sharda Sadan and the Seva Sadan. The need for women teachers became evident when girls' education was first advocated and a number of girls' schools were started. The Christian missions established in Calcutta a Normal school in 1852 for the training of Christian women teachers. In 1863, the Sarah Tucker School opened a separate department for training the future teachers. During the decade from 1867 to 1877, Mary Carpenter, a great social worker of England, visited India and induced the British government to establish a network of girls' Normal Schools in the country.

Mary opened Normal Schools for girls at Ahmedabad, Poona and Madras. In 1870, a training class was started in the Madras Mission's Day School. In 1871, Keshab Chandra Sen opened a Normal School for girls at Poona. The Arya Samaj opened a number of Normal Girls' School in Uttar Pradesh and Punjab. The Isabella Thoburn School at Lucknow and St. Anne's School at Mangalore also started Normal Training classes for girls. Besides, many other training colleges were opened at Calcutta, Madras and Shillong. The Government Training College for women was opened at Allahabad in 1945. Many co-educational institutions provided for the training of teachers. Gradually the profession of teaching began to be adopted by women of respectable families of Hindus, Muslims and other castes. In 1946-47, about 11,125 women were being trained as teachers. At present, the teachers' training programme have special significance to them.

After independence, the profession of teaching became very popular among women. There was a time when women adopted this profession under forced conditions, e.g., when they became widows or no male member was there to support them. The Indian parents saw no harm in allowing even their unmarried daughters to serve as teachers. Often they continued the profession as teachers even after their marriage and became assets to the husband's family. Women, often, taught even in co-educational institutions too.

In the twentieth century, women were found teaching at the post-graduate level in the Colleges and Universities. In no way did they lag behind the male teachers in attaining the highest academic qualifications and distinctions. They always proved better disciplinarians than men. Some of them attained the highest honour of being the Vice-Chancellors. Smt. Hansa Mehta was the first lady Vice-Chancellor. Besides many others, Miss Roma Choudhary, Vice-Chancellor, Ravindra Bharati, Calcutta and Sharda Dewan, Vice Chancellor, S.N.D.T. Women's University Bombay are remembered in the academic world to-day for their excellent work.

Besides teaching, the medical profession attracted the women most. In this field also, the Christian missions first started the experiments. Indian women rarely availed themselves the opportunity for treatment in government and missionary hospitals until women doctors and nurses took up the work. They excelled as doctors and physicians

O'Malley says that, "No amount of willingness would have made them competent to undertake professional responsibilities in colleges and hospitals had not the Christian missionaries, in face of apathy and open hostility, steadily and patiently pursued their self-appointed task of emancipation, and equipped Indian women for the responsibilities which they today are undertaking."

Some of the hospitals, employed midwives who had one year's training in nursing and midwifery and to act as a sort of attendant on the women patients in the female ward. However, the Christian missionaries, both from England and America, did pioneering work by introducing medical services to Indian women and to the Government of India. In 1866, Dr. Aitchison opened a class for 'dais' at Amritsar. The first hospital for women was opened in 1869 by the American Methodist Episcopalim Mission at Bareilly in Uttar Pradesh. Others were established shortly after, including the first Government Hospital for women at Bombay in 1866. National schemes to relieve the Indian women having various ailments began soon after. In 1885, the Countess of Dufferin's fund, popularly known as the National Association for supplying Female Medical Aid to the women of India was founded. In 1903, the Victoria Memorial Scholarships' Fund to train indigenous midwives was established. In 1918, the Lady Chelmsford League for maternity and child welfare was started with the object of training health visitors and to adopt preventive and hygienic measures. From 1885 to 1916, a network of mission hospitals spread all over the country.

The doors of medical schools in England and America had scarcely been opened to women when a few of the Indian women applied for admission. In 1866, Mrs. Anandibai Joshi qualified as a doctor in America. Unfortunately due to excessive work, she succumbed to tuberculosis and died early. A similar fate overtook Miss A. Jaganadhan of Madras who qualified as doctor in 1894 and she died the same year. The third to qualify as doctor was, Dr. Ramabai who passed in 1895 and served the country for a long time. The missionaries had already established two medical schools. One was started at Ludhiana to train Indian women as Assistant Surgeons. These women doctors were absorbed in mission hospitals in the country. The Parsee women were the first to attend a complete medical course at the Universities of Calcutta, Bombay and Madras. They studied for the degree of MBBS for a term of five years.

In 1875, the Madras Medical College and in 1883 the Bombay College opened their doors to women and since then a constant and growing supply of women doctors became available. The profession of medicine, unlike nursing, was never looked down upon. It did not carry any kind of social stigma. In 1882, the Cama Hospital, Bombay, was established by a Parsi Philanthropist on the understanding that women only would administer and form the Faculty. In the words of O'Malley, "The competence of the staff justified the deep faith of the founder and immediately won a distinguished place for the hospital and made history not only for Indian women but for medical women in western lands, where their entrance to the profession was still being very reluctantly conceded." The hospitals, universities and male practitioners showed more generous and cordial attitude to women doctors than their corresponding members had done in most of the western countries. In 1909, on the representations of the Association of Medical Women in India to the Central Committee, several improvements were made in the service conditions, including professional control of hospitals, the appointment of a women member on the Central Committee, and the formation of the Women's Medical Service in 1914. A Government subsidy of about Rs. 10,000 was paid yearly to the Countess of Dufferin's Fund for its administration. The Association of Medical Women in India submitted a memorandum for the extension of medical aid to sick women. It argued that the local governments have not provided any privileges to women of India.

The fully trained and experienced medical staff were available for the inspection of the female wards and the organizing of better means of relief for women. The yearly reports showed a steady rise in the demand for an increased amount of accommodation in the women's hospitals and the fact was that overcrowding of the sick increased every year. Due to financial stringency, some hospitals were badly equipped; some lacked in instruments and appliances, and most of them were inadequately staffed and were in need of financial assistance.

In order to fulfil the need of an institution in which a high grade medical education could be obtained under conditions which would, as far as possible, enable the students to observe the socio-religious customs of the communities to which they belonged, Lady Hardinge founded a Medical College at Delhi in 1916. Since then the Medical Schools and Colleges were opened at Agra, Lucknow, Madras and in other parts of the country. All these medical institutions gave admission to women students. Besides these, there were numerous women medical private practitioners of all castes and creed who accomplished the task of medically attending sick women and children. In the post-freedom period, the women doctors are encouraged to take service in rural dispensaries and in villages where they could readily extend their services for the benefit of humanity at large.

In the beginning, the profession of nursing was not looked on with favour by high caste Indians. Christians alone underwent this training. In 1926, the Madras Council introduced a Bill to secure the registration of nurses in that Presidency, and control their examination and work. The Central Midwife's Board of Medical Examination in Uttar Pradesh was established to set up a proper standard of training for the nurses. Some hospitals also were affiliated to conduct nurses examinations there. There was a similar Board at work for their selection as trainees. A great deal of effort to raise the standard of nursing in their respective areas was made. The Trained Nurses Association of India is affiliated with the International Council of Nurses registered under the Act of 1860. Affiliated to it was the Health Visitor's

League and the Midwives' Union. Women of all castes, colour and creed gradually changed their mentality and Nursing became a respectable profession. The spirit of service and dedication which the profession imbibed came to be recognized widely. Many women joined the courses of midwifery and training for 'Dais'. Others came out to take up the work of maternity and child welfare by becoming the health visitors. Many women work on the staff of family planning centres. During the post freedom period, Raj Kumari Amrit Kaur became Union Minister for Health and she worked most effectively for the cause of women's health and child welfare. The tradition of special care at the time of delivering the child became necessary even in the rural regions.

Another profession which attracted the Indian women was that of Lawyers. Miss Cornelia Sorabjee was the first Indian woman to pass the examination of Civil Law from Oxford University in the year 1892. She was also the first woman to obtain the LLB degree which was merely ornamental until the Legal Practitioner's (Women) Act was passed by the Government of India in 1923. Seven women qualified for the degree of LLB and became practising Lawyers during the period between 1922 and 1927.

Miss Mithan Tata started practising law in the Bombay High Court in 1924 and she emerged as a successful lawyer. The profession of law soon became quite popular among the women. The women lawyers began doing as well as the women teachers, doctors and nurses in their respective fields.

Many women took up journalism and became very successful in the field. Mrs. Swarna Kumari Debi edited *Bamabodhini Patrika*. Her daughter Sarla Debi Chaudharani edited a few magazines. Annie Besant, Sarojini Naidu, M.E. Cousins and Kamladevi Chattopadhyaya were versatile genius of pen and they contributed articles to renowned journals. Smt. Kamla Santhianadhan of Madras edited the Indian Ladies' Magazine. Mrs. Dorothy Jinarajadasa edited "Stree Dharma." Many Indian Universities ran the diploma course in Journalism where women, along with men, studied the technical course for one year to qualify as full-fledged journalists. *Nari, Manorama, Sarita, Femina, Eve's Weekly* and *The Trend* have been famous journals specially for women. Among the outstanding journalists have been Krishna Hutheesing, Padmini Sen Gupta, Frena Talwar Khan, and Shanta Rama Rau. Smt. Kusum Nair was the first to start newspaper syndicate. Many women visited USA and UK to study the new techniques of journalism. The All-India Women's Conference published its magazine *Roshni* under the supervision of women editors. Vimla Patil is a renowned journalist. Mrinal Pande has been the editor of *Hindustan* and *Kadambini*.

In the field of broadcasting, there are a number of qualified and talented women who are working as dramatists, musicians, and script writers. Smt. Mehra Masani was the first woman Station Director of All India Radio. Miss Sen Gupta was the incharge of Simla Radio Station. Many women are working as programme assistants and executives, announcers, feature writers and news readers. They work in the various departments and prove worthy of the office they occupy. Many are working in FM Radio channels with excellent performances have made their mark.

Some women managed the Jagirs and estates very efficiently after they inherited the property. They often conducted their own independent business concerns and acquired eminence. Many of them became employed in the various business concerns. They serve as Branch managers, Area managers and Business secretaries. Many women have shown better ability than men in conducting business transactions. Miss Ahama Roy has been the weaver designer in the Design Centre of the Handloom Board, Bombay;

Kumari Nalini Chambal has been the Deputy Director of Designs, and Dr. Sita Poiya has been the Assistant Manager of the Handloom Emporium. Kamla Devi Chattopadhyaya became the first President of Indian Co-operative Union. Women are taking charge of almost extinct and dying cottage industries of India and they have revived the ancient heritage in art and crafts and they are modelling them on modern lines. They also work in the sections of weaving, designing retailing and even export dealings. Smt. B.K. Nehru organized handicraft centres all over India. An export section was opened at Delhi under the guidance of Smt. Prem Berry. Indra Nooyi is one of the top CEO's of the present age.

Other top present day CEOs include Akhila Srinivasan (Shriram Investments), Chanda Kochar (ICICI Bank), Ekta Kapoor (Balaji Telefilms), Jyoti Naik (Lijjat Papad), Kiran Majumdar Shaw (Biocon), Naina Lal Kidwai (HSBC), Preetha Reddy (Appolo), Priya Paul (Apeejay Park Hotels), Rajshree Pathy (Rajshree Sugar and Chemicals), Ranjana Kumar (NABARD), Renuka Ramnath (ICICI Ventures), Ritu Nanda (Escolife), Shahnaz Hussain (Shahnaz Herbals), Sharan Apparao (Apparao Galleries), Simone Tata (Trent Ltd.), Sulajja Girodia Motwani (Kinetic), Tarjani Vakil (Exim Bank) and Zia Mody (AZB).

Women's talents have been utilized in the renowned firms like the Tata Iron and Steel Company and Delhi Cloth Mills and several other important concerns and financial institutions. Smt. Sona Baliwala, a competent and capable business woman, is the chief Publicity officer of the Tata Oil Mills. Women are showing their capabilities in the tasks of Hotel and tourism management. Courses in business administration are now becoming popular in Colleges and Universities and large number of woman are taking such courses in order to be better equipped for managing the business concerns. The new degree of MBA has been very popular with the new generation of women. The names of

Pupul Jaykar and Ms. Kamla Vatsyayan are famous for their contribution to art and crafts.

The daring among the women aspire to become pilots. Miss Prema Mathur won an international award in aviation. Many women followed the example of Miss Mathur and they are trained pilots. Besides private institutions, the Vanasthali Vidyapith conducts courses in aviation. Numerous young and attractive women have entered the career as air-hostesses not only on flights operated by the Private Airlines and Air India within India and abroad, but also on flights operated by foreign companies. They efficiently work in various offices too.

Women in rural areas assist men in the field work. They sow seeds, do weeding and assist the male members in the task of irrigation. They are seen employed in thrashing out grain and winnowing or stacking the hay. The rural women also pat the cow-dung with their hands into flat cakes to be used as fuel when dry. Women take part in the functioning of co-operative societies as members and serve occasionally on the managing committees or act as officers to these societies. Some women maintain schools and Intermediate colleges as managers. After independence, the rural women have learnt to exercise their right to vote and elect their representatives. The 30 per cent reservation to women in Panchayats and other local organizations has done miracles and the women have brought about a total metamorphosis of their own personality. Social service has been taken up by women in NGOs as service professionals.

Women of India have been working in various industries also. The women labourers used to work on tea, coffee and rubber plantations and later in textile and tobacco factories, oil-presses, etc. They also worked in large numbers in coal, iron, manganese and gold mines. The All-India Women's Conference pleaded with the government to enact legislations for protecting them from exploitation, and providing them with sanitation facilities and medical aid. They are now prohibited to work in underground mines and their working hours per day have been considerably reduced. The child welfare and maternity benefit schemes have been introduced for them. The International Labour Office at Geneva has always been in touch with the women's organizations working for social change and protection of women in various industries.

Indian women have taken active part in the film industry. In the beginning, they played different roles in the movies but with the emergence of talkies, many women started taking full-fledged roles in acting. Devika Rani and Leela Chitnis were the earliest important heroines of the film land. Nargis, Kamini Kaushal, Suraiyya, Nimmi and Meena Kumari have won laurels in the cinema industry in the post independence period. The profession of film stars is no longer looked down upon by the society. Girls from well-to-do and respectable families are joining the film industry these days. Poona Film Institute was founded to train young men and women in the art of acting. The products of this institute have won great appreciation from the public. Many heroines like Nargis, Wahida Rahman and Meena Kumari have been honoured with Padma Sri and Padma Vibhushan. We now see a very confident young woman who can face the challenge of essaying any role in films

Many outstanding women have held positions of high honour and responsibility and act as the mouth-piece for the inarticulate millions of their sex. They still hold positions in municipal committees, district boards and legislatures and serve on various educational bodies. Madras was the first in nominating a woman to the Council. She was Dr. Muthulakshmi Reddi. This came as a result of representations made by the Women's Indian Association to the Governor. Dr. Reddi's abilities and services in medicine and in social reform were already well known, and she was later appointed as the Deputy President of the Madras Legislative Council. Since then she courageously initiated legislations to abolish the system of Devdasis and was responsible for the enactment of many other useful legislations to improve the women's lot in the province. In Uttar Pradesh, a nominated member was Mrs. E. Ahmad Shah. In the Central Provinces, Anusuya Bai Kale was nominated, while in Bombay Miss I. Dickinson was nominated to the Council.

Since 1925, women have been appointed as Magistrates. Two Indian women were appointed members of Select Committees, Dr. M. Reddi to the Auxiliary Committee on Education of the Statutory Commission, and Mrs. R.B. Nehru to the Committee on Age of Consent. Raj Kumari Amrit Kaur was appointed India's Cabinet Minister for Health. Several women were appointed on important and high posts, such as Governors and Ministers. Sarojini Naidu became the first woman Governor of a state in India. Sucheta Kripalani became the Chief Minister of Uttar Pradesh. Today, there are many women Ministers in different provinces. They are also serving as Ambassadors and High Commissioners. Mrs. Vijay Lakshmi Pandit was appointed the ambassador to USA and USSR and Mrs. Margaret Alva worked as Deputy Speaker of the Lok Sabha for many years. To excel all, the Prime Minister of India was the gallant and daring lady—Smt. Indira Gandhi. She guided the country on the right path of social justice, scientific development, economic solidarity and a firm foreign policy. Under her inspiring leadership, India achieved the historic victory in the Indo-Pak War in December 1971. Mrs. Indira Gandhi represented the 'Shakti'—the true might of womanhood.

Different political parties have active women members who are shaping the policies of their respective parties with courage and foresight. The Congress Party has many veteran leaders like Sonia Gandhi, Renuka Choudhary, Sheila Dixit and Meera Kumar. Besides this, Dr. (Mrs.) Rajendra Kumari

Bajpai was the U.P. Congress President. Sucheta Kripalani and Tarkeshwari Sinha (Bihar) occupied important positions. Mrs. Shakuntla Srivastava is a leader of Socialist Party. Mrs. Renuka Ray, Mrs. Thomas and Brinda Karat, Subhashini Ali, Shyamali Gupta are some important figures in the Communist Party. With growing political consciousness women have became active and awakened citizens of India. They contest elections and assume various important roles with a determined will to serve their country with whole-hearted excellence.

There is no department of public service today where women have not entered. Women appear in different competitive examinations and come out successful. Many of them are District Magistrates, Judges and Engineers. They also serve the Indian Police services, Indian Postal Services, Indian Foreign Services and the various Provincial Services. They have entered the various government and private Banks and offices and are serving efficiently on various assignments. No sphere of public activity is untouched by the women today.

Women also take interest in voluntary social service. Early work in this sphere was almost exclusively done for the social upliftment of women such as provision of homes for destitute women, pre-natal shelters, social education centres, opening of libraries and cultural and recreational services. A recent development has been the increase in vocational training centres and arts and crafts centres aiming at making women economically independent.

Smt. Kulsum Sayani worked in Bombay and converted three lakhs women into literate persons. In Bengal, Ramola Sinha did pioneering work in the rescue of women. Pushpaben Mehta and Mridula Sarabhai worked in Gujarat. V. Lakshmi of Madras did memorable work. Mrs. Rameshwari Nehru, Smt. K. Cama, Smt. Shanti Kabir, Smt. Leelavati Munshi and Smt. Janki Devi Bajaj were eminent social workers. Many organizations like Seva Sadan and Young women Christian Association also conducted social service and trained the women for various responsible jobs.

There have also been many distinguished women artists in India. Para was a talented painter of Kangra School of Rajput Miniature Painting of the late 19th century. Swarna Kumari Debi was a gifted musician and a painter. She also wrote historical and social novels, dramas and lyrics. Smt. Leila Sokhey, friend and associate of Anna Pavlova, revived the Kathak dance. She was one of the pioneers of Indian dance and the creative Ballets. Bala Saraswati was a dancer of great repute who brought about a renaissance in Bharat Natyam style of dance. Gauri Devi, daughter of Nandlal Bose was a talented dancer who represented the Manipuri style. Rukmini Devi of Madras popularized Bharat Natyam throughout India. Among the dancers of repute were Mrinalini Sarabhai, Vaijayanthjimala, Kumari Kamla, Shanta Rao, Indrani Rahman, Sarda Sehgal, Tara Choudhary, Kumudini and Shevanti, Shirin and Roshan Vajeekadar, Vinoo Indrani, Anjali Hora, Satyavati and Kumkum Mathur—all had established themselves as dancers of quality in Bharat Natyam and Oddissi styles. Roshan Kumari, Damayanti Joshi and Rani Karna were fine exponents of Kathak. The Jhaveri sister, Nayana and Ranjan, had revived various art forms in dance. Programmes of dances are gaining popularity in the educational institutions, and girls in large numbers are actively participating in them. Lata Mangeshkar and Asha Bhonsley, the playback singers, are today admired in the world for their sweet rendering of classical and light music.

In the field of painting Amrita Shergil was the leading modern Indian woman artist. She was the first to bring a new note in modern Indian Painting by demonstrating that revivalism was not enough and one must evolve something purposeful from within oneself. She had a genius for colour, while her realism brought a living force to her paintings, which truly bear in them the spirit of India. Li Gotami—a student of Abanindra Nath Tagore and Nandlal Bose had shown special effect in portrait painting. She also reproduced the ancient style, colours and subjects found in Buddhist frescoes and murals of the monasteries of Northern Laddakh.

Sushila Yawalkar, dancer, painter and sculptress has made a name for herself. Her sculptures show clearly that they have been modelled by the hands of a painter. Premja Chaudhari is also admired for her inspirational work as a painter and sculptress. Sheroo Sidwa has been a sculptress of fame. Sheila Anden, Mary Roop Krishna and Amina Ahmad are eminent artists. These days, the art and crafts are taught in schools and colleges.

Many colours have been invented in drawing and painting schools. The Bombay Art School has popularized painting among the women, so much so that today painting has become a hobby with many middle class family girls. Painting on fabrics is also popular and the women's natural attributes towards fine arts find a full expression in the home and outside life.

During the modern period, women have been able to speak freely in their own voices as women. Swarna Kumari Debi was the first novelist in Bengali language. Sarla, her daughter, was a versatile Bengali prose writer. Every regional language in India has distinguished women writers. The voices of these women are full of faith and hope. Among the Hindi poetesses, Subhadra Kumari Chauhan and Mahadevi Verma are the most outstanding. Besides, Usha Devi Mitra, Amrita Preetam and Shivani are eminent modern novelists. Among the women who enriched English language and literature are Sarojini Naidu and Toru Dutta. Other women English writers are Bharati Sarabhai, Shanta Rama Rau, Kamla Markandeya, and many others. The number of women who are making notable contribution to literature is increasing everyday.Women contribute articles in many magazines and write short stories, one-act plays, essays, novels and they compose beautiful poetry. They are serving as editors of newspapers and magazines.

Raj Kumari Amrit Kaur set an example for North Indian women by participating in competitive tennis. Pandita Kshama Roy started serious tennis in 1920. M.E. Cousins mentions in her diary how the Maharani of Baroda, even at age of 60, played fine tennis. Today Indian women in school, colleges and Universities are provided with opportunities to play Tennis, Badminton, Basketball, Volleyball and other outdoor games. They have qualified in the various items of Sports and they participate even in the international sports events. The games most popular with the Indian women are Table Tennis, Badminton, Hockey, Cricket, Chess, and basketball. Indian women are also attracted towards athletics. In 1934, Olympics athletics was introduced on a competitive basis for women. They also participated in international athletics at the Helsinki Olympics in 1952. Mary Leela Rao is a well-known figure in the Olympic world. Sayeeda Sultana was first to become world champion in Table-tennis. In Badminton, Tara Deodhar, won the US Women's title while studying in the USA. Other names worth mentioning are Mumtaz Lotwala, Prem Parasher, S. Kapadia, S. Athavale, In Table-tennis, many Indian women like Urmila Thapar and Rita Davar won laurels. Sania Mirza is earning name and fame in tennis while Saina Nehwal is doing so in Badminton. Volleyball first became popular among women of M.P. The Bharatiya Nari Volley Ball Sangh—a pioneer body arranged for coaching the girls, and held tournaments. A few Indian women went to Moscow in 1952 to compete for the women's world championship. Indian women like P.T. Usha, Kunjarani Devi, Karnam Malleshwari and others participated in competitions at the world level and glorified the country's name. Kamaljit Sandhu became the first Indian woman to win a gold medal in Asian games.

Indian women participated in Swimming also. The unchallenged Indian queen of this sport was Dolly Nazir of Bombay who won the major swimming titles in India. She performed the marathon feat of swimming from a long distance point in the Arabian Sea to the Gateway of India in Bombay. Others in the list include Rima Datta, Mahjari Bhargava, Smita Desai, Anita Sood, Bula Choudhri, Nisha Millet and Shikha Tandon. Women are participating in various team games of Cricket, Hockey, Football and Table Tennis.

The Indian women did not take much time to come up to the level of the responsibility entrusted to them and share it equally with men. They miraculously rose to the occasion to enjoy the benefits of modern civilization. They distinguished themselves in all spheres of activity. The economic independence of women in turn brought about favourable social changes. They are now free to make their own choice of being married or remain unmarried, they have also become free to break the barriers of circular community outlook and brought about inter-caste and inter-communal marriages. All these progressive tendencies are silently entering the women's apartments. Fresh problems have, also, arisen along with their advancement towards excellence but they are daring and courageous as ever.

The recently concluded 15th Lok Sabha elections have delivered a record 59 women as members of Parliament, the highest since independence, raising their parliamentary participation to 10.7%. Seventeen of these women are under 40. India falls in the lowest quartile with respect to the number of women in parliament (9.1%) in the 14th Lok Sabha). Even Rwanda (56.7%), South Africa (44.5%), Mozambique (34.8%) and many others have much more women representatives. According to the UN's 2008 survey of women in politics, representation of women leaders at the grassroot level in India is nearly 50%, especially since the passing of the 73rd amendment of 1992, which allotted one-third of all seats to women. The panchayati raj, that bedrock of rural government, has fostered more and more women participants and leaders. Several states, including Madhya Pradesh, Himachal Pradesh, Bihar and most recently, Uttarakhand, have allotted 50% of panchayat seats for women.

Since 1998, the Constitution (84th Amendment) Bill relating to women's reservation is pending. Political parties declare avowed faith in it but do not give tickets to women to stand in elections. The country's ruling party Congress, led by a woman and supposedly pushing for reservation for women till recently, had 10 per cent of women among the candidates. For the BJP and the Communist Party of India (Marxist), the proportion of women candidates is at 7 per cent. Women have been relegated to the "women's wing" of the party, and made to concentrate on what are seen as specifically "women's issues" such as dowry and rape cases, and occasionally on more general concerns like price rise which are seen to affect especially "housewives."

Barring striking exceptions where dynastic charisma matters, women politicians have found it difficult to rise within party hierarchies. They have managed to achieve clear leadership only when they have effectively broken out and set up parties on their own. Then only there is unquestioning acceptance by the (largely male) party rank and file of the leader's decisions. But no woman politician from a rural area or from a general house has established herself. The reason is that general housewives focus on three issues: healthcare, education, and the funds to make these two things happen. In the political parties, particularly in the Hindi heartland, it will take a lot of effort to even recall the names of prominent women politicians.

Contrary to the common perception, a large per cent of women in India work. India has the world's largest number of professionally qualified women. It has the largest population of working women in the world. India has more number of doctors, surgeons, scientists, professors than the United States. As an example at software industry, 30% of the workforce is female. They are at par with their male counterparts in terms of wages, position at the workplace. The National data collection agencies accept the fact that there is a serious under-estimation of women's contribution as workers. In rural India, agriculture and allied industrial sectors employ as much as 89.5% of the total female labour. In overall farm production, women's average contribution is estimated at 55% to 66% of the total labour.

According to a 1991 World Bank report, women accounted for 94% of total employment in dairy production in India. Women constitute 51% of the total employed in forest-based small-scale enterprises. Yet, by nature and temperament a woman is at her best and happiest when she is the director of the household. She is a mother first and last. Under the pressure of growing economic complexities, she is often forced to pursue outdoor career and profession. Her life, therefore, becomes divided into two worlds. One is the outer sphere of her activities where mostly she has to work as hard as a man and in order to keep herself secure she is often forced to become rough and rude in her behaviour. The other is the household or the inner sphere of the family where she has to act as wife, mother, sister or daughter and she pursues the accommoda-ting and soft behaviour and temperament. Tired and exhausted, she knows no rest. She has to look after all other members of the family. Most of the middle class women have to do cooking, cleaning and other household duties even after they attend to their outdoor duties. All this has affected the women mentally and physically both.

Besides, the after-effects of women's coming out to serve

in different spheres have not always proved beneficial. The women who are the cultural torch bearers of the community, have still to face bitter criticism of the family and society for any progressive step they take. The wine has changed but the bottles are the same. What is required actually is a complete transformation in the outlook of men and the society both. A revival of Vedic values when women freely moved in mixed gatherings with moral courage and self-confidence and without the least aspersions from the family or the society is the call of the day.

Modern India has three unique achievements to her credit, the attainment of freedom with new techniques of truth and non-violence, the emancipation of Harijans without any major struggle and women being bestowed with equal in status in society and position with no concrete opposition from the menfolk. The women's movement, more or less, met the same fate as the national movement. In the pre-independence period, there were definite objects freedom for women and freedom for the country. Women discarded social taboos, came out to move freely in society, attained their targets in education and politics and gave excellent performance. The leaders of the Women's Movement joined the national movement, displayed their heroic capabilities and capacity to struggle hard. They achieved in no time the freedom of women and equality of status with men. They then restricted their activities only to pressurizing the government for social legislations which may or may not have any practical effect on people at large. They pressed the government to pass the Dowry Act but in vain. So was the take of other legislations related to women.

There are many educated women in India, who, in the name of modernity are ready to sacrifice even the best of their culture and tradition and become westernized butterflies. At the same time, there are numerous women still living under medieval notions and superstitions. They observe purdah, worship 'pret' (the evil spirits), love jewellery more than their life and nourish blind faith. As such the women of India constitute an interesting gathering where different types of women with typical notion and faith are represented at large. It is not only true for India but for the women of many countries.

The women's organizations which exist today are mostly narrow in scope and nature. Either they are for serving the poor women in earning their livelihood or they are Clubs for entertainment for the upper class women. There is no well defined programme for these organizations. Most of them have become inactive and obsolete as the women members complain of lack of time and avoid meeting even once a month. Most of the Ladies Club restrict their activities to chess and card-playing or organizing tambolas and kitty. The middle class women who are serving in various professions actually do not get time to join the organizations. The lower class women who are busy in washing, drying, cooking, grinding grain, drawing water, cleaning and tailoring have to face the hard realities of life and have no relief from the drudgery of life.

The Indian feminist movement did not broaden its scope after the attainment of political rights for women in free India. Ignorance still reigns supreme among the women masses. Every election finds some women worshipping the ballot boxes before casting votes. Nothing spectacular has been done to remove superstition, to educate women so as to enable them to change with the changing times and to create a sense of self-confidence in the women masses. As such, the movement definitely started shrinking and began following a policy of non-commitment in women's affairs. The lack of a well organized programme for changing the lot of the women masses and the indifference of women leaders towards the changed social problems definitely need the attention of the educated modern women.

Undoubtedly, Indian feminist movement exhibited features which are in marked contrast with its counterpart in the West. The women of the West had to face enormous difficulties in conducting their movement because their menfolk were not very keen to give them equal status in society. The men of the West felt that their women were putting them to disgrace and contempt by 'speaking' in public. Women, there, had to suffer severe terms of imprisonment for the cause of women's suffrage. In India, the cause for women's freedom was first espoused by the enlightened male members themselves. The women came upon the scene much later. Because of the traditional regard for womanhood, the Indian women effortlessly secured many democratic rights and social freedom. They were given the rights as liberally as if they were given free grants. As these rights have been secured as gifts and not found as the result of any gigantic effort, their rights still persist as liberties whose real implication is not even comprehended by the vast majority of womanhood.

The Women's Movement in India meant the furtherance of the cause of womanhood and the recognition of their merit full and complete. Unlike the women's movement in the West, the Indian feminism, did not take the form of insensate craving to acquire man's outlook, man's ambitions, man's freedom and man's power. Referring to the women's movement in the West, A.R. Wadia writes, that the very outlook of West has been to transcend femininity and its tendency is to achieve an independence, which on the one hand leads to a duplication of the virtues and the defects of man, and on the other to the production of an asexuality suicidal for the race. The feminist ideals of the West are foreign to the spirit of Indian feminism. During the course of its progress, the leaders of the women's movement in India ever kept in mind the ancient ideals and values of Indian culture, the high spirituality and the spirit of service and devotion that woman indeed symbolizes.

There is no doubt about the fact that the Indian women's role and contribution yielded the desired results. The definitions of Indian womanhood have vastly changed "from ignorance to knowledge and perfection" which ultimately became responsible for their excellence in every project. They worked hard to prove themselves in every field of life and their efforts have brought laurels to them from all over the world.

11. Conclusion

If we wish to really understand the concept of modern feminism in the present world, it is necessary to realize the highly selective development of world economy. In the new global system, there exist incredible social and economic diversities. In the women's conferences organized at the world level like Conference of Women Linking for Change in 1995; Beijing Conference on Women in 1995 and Conference on Women's Day on Food in 1996, the issue of the impact of globalization on women was sincerely deliberated upon. They admitted that the uneven development including the selective process of capitalist expansion provided a framework which might give us a comprehensive analysis of women's wage and non-wage work. With reference to women's movement, the world events of the twentieth century, specially of its last two decades, show that women faced increased economic pressures as they assumed more and more responsibilities in the course of time. The women organizations and the informal social action networks became closely linked to solve the women's issues in the present scenario.

In the 21st century, feminism emerged as the expression of a cultural identity with differences in a diverse world and it worked for global transformations of women's work under different systems and in different countries. Women have bridged the social spheres of house-holding by continuous activity organizing the social relations that generate from wage and non-wage work. They became reproducers of labour all over the world. The modern women are no more unaware of significant global events but primarily they are affected by family welfare policies. Women rose together with a call to fight against exploitation at the global level. The Asian Women Human Rights Council met in Tokyo in 1994 to hold an open tribunal on 'Traffic in women', a common evil in almost all countries.

We can easily discern that in the 21st century, the vast gap between rich and poor is increasing though it was predicted that globalization would eventually level out the economic disparities. It has resulted in highly polarized gender relations too. After Women's Year and Women's Decade, many international conferences were held in different countries to explore the real meaning and worth of feminism. Indian women also began to share the new vision. They demanded their basic rights along with the knowledge of their duties. Women in many countries of the world began fighting for individual autonomy, freedom and equality. C.E. Martin, an author of global repute, asserts about the women of USA that 'Women began their movement with the suffragists. They philosophized and organized themselves since late 1800 till 1930, when they primarily focused on the legal enactments and moral changes to gain more power and autonomy. The second wave of feminism was concerned with the social and psychological liberation. This wave was most active from 1960 to 1970. Women felt that their hearts are pumping with new feminist blood and their minds are the most educated in history and they are formulating visions of what feminism will be in the 21st century.'

In USA, this movement had the seeds in the anti-slavery movement. The abolitionist women became politically aware of their own legal oppression and they argued for women's rights on the grounds of self ownership. They believed that every human being, simply by being human, had an equal right to his or her own body and the women too deserve equality under just laws for they also equally labour hard. Their rhetorics did not impress Indian women at large but it definitely presented an alternative model of development.

The idea of a powerful woman in fact was deeply included in the Indian patriarchal culture through religion, historical circumstances and value-based system of Indian life. Indian women were provided with traditional cultural spaces at the very dawn of civilization: The western feminine model presents the individual self while the individual is normally considered to be just a part of the 'social collective' in India. Mutual cooperation and goodwill as well as the greater good of mankind have been considered very important in this country, since the dawn of civilization. There are multiple patriarchies in India and there have also been multiple types of feminism. Indian feminism survived only by its awareness of historical and cultural realities. In India, feminism meant 'an awareness of women's impression and exploitation in society at work and within the family and a conscious action by women and men, both, to change the situation.' It is why the status and position of women in India have been changing from time to time. It stands for a continuous voyage towards the ideal destination. During the tenure of strong kings and rulers, peace prevailed in the country and the Indian women enjoyed a comparatively safe place in society. During decentralized and disturbed political situations, their status and position suffered a set-back. The sages and seers of this country advised the people to respect women. Since then it became an Indian tradition to give respect to women in family and society. Whenever there was education and comparative prosperity in society men and women lived happily. Women were always respected except in the 'dark' periods of history, when political chaos, social turmoil and economic turbulence were the order of the day

In the dark period of 18th century, Indian women lived as 'subordinates and slaves'. Their own self-consciousness had disappeared. The impact of West in the 19th century India proved to be a source of inspiration to restore the principles of equality, democracy and individual rights to them. The call for changing the 'fortune' of Indian women came through the men reformers who endeavoured to uproot the socio-religious evils affecting women prevailing in the then society. The second phase of women's uplift came from the educated women themselves, when they strongly organized themselves and demanded legal enactments for their betterment. They joined various female institutions and organizations at national and international level. Gandhiji encouraged them and legitimized their participation in the national struggle of India. Many other national leaders widened the women's horizon directing them to join the non-violent and peaceful resistance under the banner of Indian National Congress. The emergence of female institutions like All India Women's Conference, National Federation of Indian Women and Women's Indian Council, puzzled the foreigners when they saw the India women with and without Purda, educated and uneducated, struggling valiantly against the tyranny of British rule. They had exhibited their inner strength and intense patriotism. For the love of motherland they sacrificed every comfort and daringly faced every challenge. After the attainment of India's freedom and establishment of self-rule, their worth was well recognized. They were easily granted equal rights in the pages of Constitution of free India.

The Constitution-makers were liberal and thoughtful enough to offer the Indian women equal and constitutional rights as free, equal and democratic citizens of India. After the Women's Year in 1975, the role of Indian women increased and expanded in every field of activity. With a critical awareness they availed the right to education in democratic India.

Programmes of their uplift were included in every Five Year Plan of the Indian government. The Ministry of Women and Child Development was constituted to look after their security and welfare. Indian women, too, availed every opportunity for their education and training. The British Government had granted to them the Property rights as early as 1874 so that they could act as the Regent and Guardians to manage the estates of their minor sons. It spread a new current of awareness and confidence in them.

It becomes necessary to cross the boundaries to study the women's work and movements. The women, today have formed national and international unions to increase wages and other facilities. They meet and discuss together their problems global level. They feel that all nations and regions must get the benefit of the social awareness and economic prosperity. The struggles of contemporary women are related to different aspects of socio-economic life in diverse contexts often arising from work based situations. In terms of pay scale, options and opportunity, the women are still being discriminated against and yet they are still endeavouring to touch the top. Only two percent qualified women in India are given high economic and educational posts. Many women organizations are working afresh to preserve the resources for future and deal with the problems of health, security and the menace of terrorism. The grass root feminism in India demands for more caring and sharing attitude and a cooperative based economic structure. The Self Employed Women's Association (SEWA) of Lucknow, Uttar Pradesh, provides a comprehensive model for sincere efforts to fulfil the women's economic, social and family requirements.

In many countries of the world, the feminist educators give lectures about the real effects of the stepped up corporate invasions. The ongoing corporate commercialization deeply penetrated the women's world too. When workers suffer from the consequences of the low wages and unhealthy social treatment how could they dream of enjoying equality and justice? The Indian Government and the NGO's are making efforts to provide to them legal support and moral force for their cause.

It is beyond doubt that the women workers have bridged the social spheres of the house-hold and outside world. They have enabled many of their counterparts to be like them. The feminists in India have done hard work by encouraging the women of their country to arise, awake and march on the path of peace, progress and prosperity. It is very sad that they still have to fight for autonomy, freedom, tolerance, non-violence and equality. They stand against all domestic violence, stereo-typed genders, sexuality, sexism, objectification, patriarchy, etc. They desire to know more and more about abortion and divorce, and they desire to acquire control of their female body. They wish to be educated and trained in different skills just as they aspire for equal privileges with men under national policies.

The European and American women also joined the feminist movement. They had become organized and had full faith in making collective efforts for the betterment of their life. They demanded rights to ensure legal and institutional changes in order to fulfil their real mission. They also demanded social and psychological liberation for themselves. For the women leaders, their personal world, name and fame and their ideology were indeed meaningful to them. There were also stay-at-home mothers who sacrificed careers to pursue more of the personal values. Many entrepreneurs and career women rose through their own merit. They had refused and rejected to be the 'victories' of the rich and powerful. Their persistent demand was always total equality and gender justice.

The new goals of women's life have ever been chosen to remove all discriminative laws, to take personal responsibility of their own decisions and to open talks about vital issues linked up with women like abortion, divorce and security of their physique and honour. As already stated, the anti-slavery movement encouraged them to be politically aware of their own legal oppressions. Women of USA asked the men to take 'their feet off their neck'. The seeds of feminism in USA and Europe were sown by their agitation to ensure "equal pay for equal work" and to end all discriminatory laws in employment and social order. They demanded full protection at their work place. In contrast, the Indian women desired and preferred to live under the system of family even if they worked and toiled independently.

In the years from 1960 to 1970, some of the feminists in Europe and USA desired to discard the notions of impropriety. Betty Friden was the leader of the second wave of feminism in USA. Under her philosophy, women urged the burning of 'bra' and demanded radical rights. At a later stage, they demanded more protection against oppression by men. They asserted that 'men and women are separate and politically antagonistic classes, due to the patriarchal state and free market system.' They asserted for gender justice as a class and believed that, "women make the best decision for themselves and they must be given legal sanctions for it."

Before 1920, the women of USA could not be the legislators, the members of jury and the judges. They had no freedom outside the work-place. They asserted that forced sex in marriage should be considered as 'rape'. They demanded access to birth-control techniques and other such informations. The 19th Amendment was passed in USA guaranteeing them the right to vote. Feminism in these countries had some deep grievances and they continuously made hectic efforts to uproot the social discrimination against them.

On the other hand, there were other women, who desired equal facilities for education and refinement. They desired genuine equality of sex. The vision of modern feminists is that both men and women must be the most authentic selves in the world. Woman must learn to deftly handle the conflicts in a healthy and assertive way and they must be aware enough to take care of themselves. They also believed in leading a more fulfilling, ethical and joyful life characterized by healthy and genuine relationship.

Women, all over the world, now feel that a new feminist blood runs deep inside them. They have been able to visualize their real progress and genuine metamorphosis in the 21st century. They have confirmed their faith in the success of feminist movement in modem times. The promise of a better future encourages the new generation of women to prefer independent living with equality and justice.

The women of modern India genuinely experienced the new fragrance of women's liberty and equality. The fresh air has reached through the windows of their awakened apartments, from palaces to huts. Yet they have adopted a cautious approach to their problems. Indian women uphold that Indian feminism is no more the expression of merely the cultural differences persisting in the diverse world. They are in fact guided by higher philosophy of life, governed by institutions of household. Indian women today are not only the awakened citizens of the country but the conscious members of the global community.

The modern Indian women do care more for their health and safety. They also care for the health of their children. They are working in institutions like 'Sewa' and 'Lijjat Papad' and innumerable self help groups. They are even working in organised trade unions to improve their economic position. The change in the life-style of Indian women may appear to be slow. The average middle class Indian women have avoided aping the life-style of the western women. Their education is no more limited to 8% or 18% but at present it covers 54.5% of' the women population and they are determined to improve it further. They are craving to acquire more technical and vocational education. Quite a good percentage of them are' employed in different fields at par with men. The Government of India is making efforts for their larger participation in all walks of life. They have joined services in Police and Army. They have joined the management services as well as they have taken high posts in the business fields. India, in fact, has not been able to improve the levels of good governance as a result that lawlessness hampers the speed of their progress. Women are exposed to various new risks and dangers. Terrorism is creating unsafe situations all over the world. Women are working in institutions like Rape crisis centres, Campaign groups and Trauma centres. They are working in Panchayats and schools. The credit for it goes to Late Sri Rajeev Gandhi, who personally saw his mother's struggle in politics and realized the difficulties of Indian women. Women have joined all the major Indian political parties, today. They are working as the office bearers and members in their organizations. Besides, there are many strong women's self supporting organizations and NGOs who are working for women's upliftment.

The regional scholars on women's issues have often concentrated upon the problems of their regions or political dogmas. It is indeed true that, the efforts of women themselves for their own resurgence have been quite remarkable. Today, highly qualified women are available in modern India for any constructive and creative work. They have presented quality literature and also earned prestigious awards including high name and fame.

The Indian local and regional women's ameliorative plans have been amazingly knitted together in a strong bond of unity and integrity. The fact remains that the feminist leaders of India have common objectives and issues and their representation in various national and International Conferences and Seminars have been indeed commendable.

The efforts of Indian women are bringing favourable results in the field of art and handicrafts. In modern India, they have joined Radio, T.V. and Films in large numbers. They have successfully joined jobs in big business houses. They are working in all the three branches of Indian army. They are prominent in the IT sector, Banking and even in share-trading. The modern scenario of women in India gives a very convincing reflection of their glowing future.

Yet there are problem areas especially in the rural sector. There have been no personal efforts on the part of our political leaders to speed up the process of development among the women masses. The urban educated women have, of course, come out of their houses to work. The discouraging features have been the increase in the crime-graph against women. It is tragic that rape, sexual harassment and exploitation at the work-place and dowry deaths still persist. Even women tourists belonging to different foreign countries have fallen prey to rape and murder here.

Still, it is very commendable that modern Indian women bother about the issue of human development specially freedom from hunger, disease and the growing clutches of terrorism. Their priorities have been education, equal opportunity and liberal treatment. They feel the need of proper child development and especially there is awareness for the protection of girl child. They are combining in self-help groups and new entrepreneurship. They desire quality education, vocational skill and they demand with one voice to end all sorts of violence against women. The Indian Government passed the law against domestic violence in 2006 which is being revised and improved. The Government also legislated for the empowerment of women in 2002. These efforts are now yielding results.

With the extension of the frontiers of knowledge and work for uplifting Indian women and their ever-increasing involvement in public life, the peculiar crimes against them have also risen. Pornography, videography and phone cameras have been misused as the new instruments of the exposition of privacy, molestation and rape. The criminals are creating and selling explicit sexual images which have not been as yet, covered under any criminal law. The changing relations between gender and sexuality, the sexist advertisements or obscene films and film songs are degrading the present environment. The Beauty contests are getting global popularity but there is controversy over depicting the women as an object and not as a human being with heart and mind within her.

In some states of India, where there are now female Chief Ministers, crimes against women have not yet stopped. Women in rural and urban regions are often beaten and exploited. The conscious citizens of India are worried and they want change. Clear is the fact that the laws, if framed, are just alive on papers only. Unless the mode of thinking of people changes women shall always be victimized. The status and position of Indian women was far better in the hoary past of Indian history when their role in the family and society were well defined and they were quite useful and productive members of society. Women must learn to think about themselves and be self-reliant. They must be aware enough to take decisions themselves.

For their regeneration and resurgence and for the amelioration of the problems in their life, the successful women must strive hard to guide and help their kind. If they have reached the zenith of their career and have performed successfully, they must encourage other women to do so. What is urgently required is a change in the attitude of the members of the family towards them. When the society in general and the men in particular, come to possess high regards and a decent attitude towards them, the modern Indian women would become equal citizens of India in the real sense of the term. The men must undergo the process of a psychological change and in it mothers and grandmothers have a special role to play.

Indians have inherited the social arrangements based on the household priorities organized by gender and age and maintained through family roles. The colonial interest lay in maintaining the same old social pattern as that facilitated easy revenue collection for them. The women's exclusive work at home and the increased control over them gave the men a clear autonomy in domestic domain too. This pattern has now drastically changed and the modern Indian women have been successfully marching ahead on the road to awareness not only to enjoy their rights but to perform their duties too.

Women have not only been granted legal access to equality under the Constitution of 1950 but they enjoy an all round freedom of education and refinement, justice and the fruits of all the welfare activities. The golden knot of mutual relationship keeps them tied together with the institution of family which is approved by religion and admired by the Indian seers and sages. The system of patriarchy, to-day, does not mean the dominant authority of the men over women of the household. Within the framework of the patriarchal system, Indian women have been assigned the necessary freedom and social equality. For lack of education, they had to suffer much in the past. Today, when they have been granted equality with men under constitutions, they are enjoying the fruits of their own hard work and merit. In theory, there have always been no bars to obstruct their path to glory, grandeur and greatness. Through their hard and meritorious work, they are marching toward with enough satisfaction. In reality they quite realize that there is still a lot for them to be achieved. Women have realized the fact that they must be true to their own conscience and live a worthy and moral life. Their duty is to spread the light of self-awareness among their counterparts too.

It shall not be wrong to assert that in modern India, there are no more women's issues which await a prompt solution but there indeed, are the socio-economic questions which deserve the immediate attention of the government and the decision-makers on national level and every citizen of India, men and women both.

Index